Business SOS™

The Fallout of a Pandemic

What Washington and Wall Street

Can't or Won't Do for Us

We Have to Do Ourselves

Book II

BY: DEBORAH J SCARPA
AUGUST 1, 2020

I dedicate this book to my longest and dearest friend
Carol Kauffman without whose never-failing
encouragement and constant reminders that timing is
sometimes our most important catalyst to success.

Business SOS™

Fallout of a Pandemic

Book II

Introduction

Chapter 1 Our State of Shock

The Triple Systematic Bombshell of COVID-19

Chapter 2 How Business and Life Has Changed Forever

Where is the New Normal?

Chapter 3 Partnerships and Integration

A Collective Big Think!

Chapter 4 Our New Business Environment

Sweatpants Executives

Smaller Offices, Home Offices, and

Remote Work. It Works!

Chapter 5 Advanced IT, Digital Marketing, and AI are for

Small Businesses

Without Them, You Will Not Survive!

Chapter 6 Bankruptcy is Not for Small Businesses

There are Fangs in These Laws and It is

Expensive, Go Figure

Chapter 7 The Road Map to Your Future

A New Wave Business Plan

Chapter 8 Broken or Broken Open?

A Sound Way Forward

Conclusion

Introduction

To the shock of the world, a deadly pandemic has arrived and, even though there was some preparedness, no one could have foreseen the absolute celerity with which this virus has travelled and spread across the world in a very short time. Total economic destruction and a complete systematic breakdown have occurred as an added catastrophe to this scourge. The COVID-19 pandemic has emerged, becoming the single greatest threat to business durability in history, and could remain so for at least 18 months. Limited applicable research and very little has been written thus far about this virus and its effect on small business. Companies need to develop alternate plans to slow the pandemic's progress and limit its impact on employees, shareholders, partners, consumers, and communities. This will require more than merely double-checking the soundness of existing business plans. This, in fact, is Business SOS™ at its pivotal moment in history. The severity of the pandemic is an existential threat to all of our lives and the life of our economy as we knew it a few months ago.

I want to believe that my past experiences have prepared me to take on these new challenges and provide help to my small business brothers and sisters. I am writing this second edition to Business SOS™ with that purpose in mind. In my first book, I mentioned that, when you face financial catastrophe, you react physically by exhibiting symptoms of high anxiety, such as sleepiness, depression, and nervousness; however, with a life-threatening pandemic, your reaction is all visceral. I am fearful for myself, my family, and the country.

Current models developed by the Harvard Business School suggest that this "pandemic is likely to come in three waves, with each wave sweeping across the globe in a matter of weeks and lasting as long as three months."[i]

They detail the need to make a shift in your business plan, away from protecting your infrastructure and toward protecting your employees and their ability to conduct business during a sustained crisis. In addition, you need to create adaptability for your business so that you can assess and evaluate whether your business model(s) are viable in a post-pandemic environment. Perhaps some models aborted totally.

Health is a critical issue for businesses. We can easily assume that a vaccine will not arrive anytime soon, even in the most optimistic circles. If they develop antivirals and other drug treatments, they will be in short supply. Now that we are pouring viral drugs in overuse and sometimes abusive fashion, we will develop resistance, which will cause additional health problems down the road. When a vaccine is developed, there may not be enough for many months, some speculating as far away as 2022, which will cause shortages and distribution problems. Therefore, contingency planning by forward-looking companies is imperative. With the right mix of resources we can survive.

A business isolated in quarantine must be coordinated by a smart pandemic or crisis team that taps into key functions, including business model assessment, human resources, operations, security, legal counsel, communications, marketing, and technology. This planning focuses on medical and nonmedical risk-mitigation strategies to reduce infection personally and with/by staff as well as maintain business stability and continuity, while reassessing threats in real-time.

As of the writing of this book, we are in phase two and three in a variety of regions depending on the level of spread. Lockdown and mitigation with a slowly phased plan for reopening were aborted when the economic recovery began to be as critical a problem to the health and welfare of each citizen as the virus. The time for planning has long passed since any plans will have needed to already have been implemented. According to the CDC and the Presidential Task Force, it looks as though there could be sustained, systematic disruption to most small businesses for the next two to four years. In the complex and uncertain environment of a sustained, evolving crisis, the most robust organizations will not be those organizations that simply have plans in place, but those organizations with continuous sensing and response capabilities. As Darwin noted, the most adaptive species are the fittest.[ii]

This pandemic will continue to impact almost every part of our lives. However, significant opportunities will occur for existing and startup companies to leverage opportunistic or longer-term goals for the growth of their businesses and current or new revenue streams will arise from new environmental and ecosystem changes. Here is my take on both.[iii]

Yes, there is a demand for delivery services as well as medical and cleaning crews. Most of us could not imagine how difficult those business models are to manage and control. Until last month, many of us have relied too heavily on the person-to-person overtures and not enough on the remote solicitation and servicing of our business capabilities. Now is the time to examine the viability of this technology. I will spend much time in this book, explaining how most businesses can now harness these structural changes to fit most companies' execution of critical aspects.

With little or no resistance, we welcomed the new normal of working with remote applications. Businesses have now learned how to utilize remote working tools and applications that provide value while cutting overhead costs. The myriad of remote working applications and solutions will be the saving grace of the entire pandemic, from ordering food, masks, disinfectant to specialized marketing services and lead generation to even more significant growth in e-commerce sites. It is now time to embrace automation fully. Below are some of the newer services popping up that can be used as examples.

The hardest thing for me was to stop going to the gym. Once we were given the stand in place orders by the governor, I regretted not making that third room into a gym. One of the fastest-growing sectors is remote access to fitness. As the coronavirus continues to spread, fitness studios around the country are keeping their doors closed and adjusting to a new reality. Even SoulCycle is adapting by offering its cycling studio bikes for pre-order with a price tag of $2,500, with the company saying it will release on-demand virtual classes later this year. The whole notion of a "virtual" trainer will now explode into other exercise modalities as well. Recently they were offering classes with financing.[iv]

We are all worried about cybersecurity. Now that we are online constantly shopping and accessing banking information, we are more vulnerable than ever before. When you work remotely, all of the standard applications will come under cyberattacks. Just ask Zoom, which has demonstrated inferior cybersecurity firewalls. Building better versions of either applications or browser-based secure solutions will gain new levels of funding from investors, and we will see additional products storm the marketplace. Let us hope that companies like Microsoft and

Amazon do not gobble up more of the mainstream by seeing these new opportunities before small start-ups take full advantage.

I speak to digital clients every day. It was not that long ago that many of them did not see the need to have e-commerce built into their sites. This pandemic, while probably a death blow to physical retail stores, will accelerate e-commerce. PetSmart, Chewy, and Dog.com, the online pet stores, have seen an explosion of orders in recent months. E-commerce will never look back, and even more niche e-commerce opportunities will surface. These niche opportunities are gold mines waiting for those serial entrepreneurs who can brave new challenges. Now is the time, so it is not all bad news for business.[v]

Categories like entertainment are in turmoil. Is this the final act of movie theatres? Will major sports brands like the N.F.L., MLB, N.B.A., and N.H.L. finally accelerate virtual reality programming? Gaming has accelerated in this crisis. Netflix, Hulu, and Amazon Prime Video have seen a tremendous rise in viewership. Investors will be backing next-generation companies that can bring entertainment to the masses on a one-to-one basis.

This moment is for the innovator and entrepreneur who can problem-solve and study the situation with fortitude. It is for the individuals who can test and move on with unique flexibility and durability under the toughest financial and health calamity in over 100 years.

Here I go again, but, this time, I am not blindsided like I was in 2008. The economy is in convulsions. Never before in the history of this nation have, we been asked to completely shutter in. The economy had to be completely turned off, except for essential products and services. The coronavirus pandemic has sent the country's economy into a free fall. A record 30 million Americans have applied for unemployment assistance in the past three months. Now with a slow reopen, we see more unemployment applications, but we also see job growth.[vi]

Two significant federal government initiatives designed to get relief to small businesses have been initiated, each of which was part of the massive CARES Act. The launch of the first bill has been confusing and chaotic but is on the road to correction through experience. The other has been a complete debacle.

There are 30.2 million or so small businesses in the U.S. Small businesses create more than 65 percent of all new jobs. The rollout of these programs has been very chaotic.

If the administration of these programs doesn't radically improve quickly, if they are not made much more straightforward for small business owners to navigate, and if Congress doesn't appropriate additional funds, small businesses may fall into unwanted bankruptcy. The unemployment rolls will continue to grow, and the cake will be baked for prolonged economic calamity. This is America, and quantitative easing will undoubtedly be another tool utilized to get us through the worst of times.[vii]

One of the initiatives is the $350 billion Paycheck Protection Program (P.P.P.), the rules for which were promulgated by the Treasury Department and the Small Business Administration (S.B.A.). Funds are routed through banks and other lenders, including fintech firms. The other initiative is an expanded Economic Injury Disaster Loan (EIDL) program, controlled by the Small Business Administration. Under the CARES Act, businesses can receive up to $10,000 in emergency grants while their loans are in process. Both programs have proven to be cumbersome, too bureaucratic, and too slow to release funds to small business applicants.[viii]

The EIDL has almost completely broken down. The Wall Street Journal reported that nearly four million businesses have applied for funding, seeking $383 billion. In comparison, Congress has allocated less than $17 billion. These EIDL loans can be as long as 30 years in length in amounts up to $2 million at low-interest rates. The average request is $250,000, but the S.B.A. is capping loans at $15,000 and the $10,000 grants, which are supposed to be issued within three days, aren't getting too small businesses, either. Loans are so delayed that they're mostly A.B.D.: After Business Death.

On the P.P.P. front, Treasury Secretary Steve Mnuchin sold the program as a simple one, allowing banks to process loans on the same day for which they're applied. That's not happening. At least not yet. Bankers and other lenders are doing everything possible to issue these loans, which are forgivable for up to two months of operating costs for payroll, at up to $100,000 per worker. The P.P.P. loans are capped at $10 million. Hotels and restaurants that have suffered, unlike during any other period in history, can tap into the P.P.P. on a per-location basis. The P.P.P. can be used for rent and utilities, too, but 75% must be for payroll to be forgivable. Significant improvements to both programs are needed immediately.[ix]

First, a concerted effort must be made to streamline the entire process for both programs, allowing for a simple authentication process from businesses and the straightforward, risk-free ability for lenders to disburse funds as long as no blatant fraud is detected. Banks need to be able to do their jobs with as little red tape as possible if the federal government expects the country's banking system to be the disbursement mechanism for these funds.

Second, speed and ease are everything here. It's excellent that 880,000 loans totaling more than $215 billion have already been approved, but the funds need to get out ASAP. That loan applications need to be manually entered into the S.B.A.'s E-Tran loan portal and that each one can take 25-75 minutes is evidence of significant room for improvement.

Third, for borrowers who don't have a lending relationship with their bank, Congress should find alternative options. If the Department of Treasury can issue direct cash assistance to American households, couldn't it do the same thing for small businesses? If not the Treasury, then state departments of revenue could serve as conduits. Both have the needed information to move money and prevent fraud. Fourth, Congress should appropriate more funds until all businesses that have been hurt get the relief they need. We don't dole out unemployment insurance based on the order of application until the funds run out, and we shouldn't do it with small business support.

Thirty percent of the U.S. economy is being forced to hibernate to keep the American people safe. The P.P.P. and EIDL programs have the vital goals of keeping employees connected to employers, while better positioning businesses to gear up when things thaw out, and companies can reopen in phases. These programs can keep people off of the exploding unemployment rolls, but significant reforms must be enacted.[x]

Even the most intrepid executive, entrepreneur, or freelancer would be forgiven for struggling to adapt to a global pandemic.[xi]

The impact of the coronavirus has been unrelenting: hospitals at capacity, students sent home, conferences cancelled, inventory sold-out, markets in free fall, and cities under lockdown. It is a lot to digest. I, for one, have gone through the seven stages of death to my business model in 2008, but I have been able to adjust to this new SOS environment. This time many of us did not leverage our homes and businesses, and most of us adopted "an anything can happen" attitude after the last shock. So, I am hoping that we can better adapt to the rapid changes that are occurring as I write this manuscript because this is not human-made.

This moment requires us to learn new skills, develop new habits, and let go of old ways of working. In the book *Range*, there's a chapter about "dropping familiar tools" that explains how experienced professionals will overlearn specific behaviors and then fail to adapt to new circumstances. This mentality affects everyone from firefighters to aviation crews to NASA engineers, often with deadly results, and underscores how hard it can be to adapt to change.[xii]

Experts are saying now that cases may peak in August to December, which means that everyone should be hunkering down for 12 or more weeks of social distancing and isolation. A COVID-19 vaccine just started human trials, but testing in large enough sample sizes to identify side effects and then ramping up large-scale production still might not be fully available for more than a year. In other words, dealing with this virus is not a sprint; it's a marathon. A marathon no one signed up for.[xiii]

My brother, Dean, is a brilliant entrepreneur and an Ironman Triathlon participant. Still, even he is stalled in his once-thriving business. He has been an inspiration to me, but I can hear the frustration and utter incredulity in his voice. As any path forward is a total leap of faith in times of crises, many of my readers from book one quickly found their way out of the 2008 crisis. I am hopeful this situation will be the same for COVID-19. The Great Recession now seems minor compared to this encompassing global apocalypse.

However, these two mega disruptions are now just within a decade. They are nightmarish because they not only include our economic health but our very survival. It seems like we are on a trend of being out of one mess into another. The good thing for me is that I feel compelled to develop a way forward for myself, family, friends, and readers through the concept of Business SOS™ This network will provide much-needed support to small businesses everywhere. This will be based on authentic American values of helping ourselves by helping each other with ethics and honor. This move from our norms to work with governments or entities that do not have compatible value systems is why we are in the mess we are in, so suddenly after the last crisis. Let's face it; large multinational companies made fortunes in the previous TARP bailouts. It is well-documented that many companies used the money for stock buybacks. This helped shareholders, but not Main Street. We need to bring manufacturing back to America at a much faster pace during this pandemic. I will discuss how this can be done with new capital resources and the will to succeed.

I have discovered several essential alternatives, methods, and resources for supporting "how we can help ourselves by helping each other" and will outline them in this new book. Taking alternative courses of action and completely rethinking how to retool all aspects of business is what allowed me to re-launch my own business and can be the mechanism to help millions of others who have found themselves in the same situation. After the 2008 debacle, there does not seem to be enough preparedness for new challenges, so we are left high and dry once again to think it through. It will take utter grit and massive creativity to reach for the path that will restart our economy, and most of the businesses now in lockdown.

Business SOS™ neither pretends to be a magical cure-all, nor should it be. What Business SOS™ does promote, is innovative, specialized, and sustainable solutions for struggling small businesses.

Each small business is unique and needs specialized attention and resources, which led to the development of the Business SOS™ Network. As the following pages will describe, this interactive network can form the foundation for the launch or re-launch of many small businesses, even during a sustained global pandemic and while in isolation. It may be the moment when we can walk and chew gum at the same time. We are creating new consumer habits at quantum speed. This book will take you through my step-by-step process for my own business while outlining a way to think through your current business model to see if it is sustainable with adjustments or if it is time to reinvent your skill level. Like anything, if you look at it negatively, it is a ball and chain. If you see it as a unique historic challenge, then it can be most rewarding. For one, I was glued to the news media in the last crisis, and it affected me and the speed by which I was able to adjust. I suggest you listen to the CDC Guidelines and take the pundits on any side of the aisle with a grain of salt. Remember, they are a business in

the same crisis trying to keep their audiences glued to the

T.V. or mobile device. Please get away from this situation

and spend each moment thinking about how to take your

business to the next level despite the pandemic.

Chapter 1

Our State of Shock

The Triple Systematic Bombshell of COVID-19

Usually, economic storms are the result of demand shocks, such as 9/11; supply shocks, like the oil crisis; or financial crises, like the fall of Lehman Brothers. Today, we are faced with all three horrible economic catastrophes and a world health crisis that we still do not understand or have a treatment for as of this publication. Even though this perfect storm of economic downturns is happening, we need to find the human reserves to navigate to a solution as soon as possible. With only essential workers working, how do we stop the whole system from imploding and bringing us all down? These are stressful times, but we must execute big thinking across the globe as, without exaggeration, humanity is at stake. Business owners stay up all night worrying as they try to save themselves from financial ruin, often forgetting that they must protect themselves and their staff daily from a deadly virus as well. We are all sick of quarantine, and it gets harder each day to treat all aspects of your life from your automobile, office, and home as a clinical laboratory. We have read that the source of the virus may have been the result of an accident in a highly specialized virology laboratory in Wuhan. So, if a trained technician or doctor gets it wrong, the chances that we can sustain a vigilance at that level is not realistic. As work has always been my friend, it is a great psychological healer for me to focus on the challenges at hand, in this case, to re-tool one's business to survive this situation.

I tried to be very humble in expressing my observations in the first Business SOS™ book. One of the most differential moments was the realization that most of us have no idea of the systematic risk we take in a digitally globalized world while running our small businesses. Who would have thought that a flu-like disease in a region of China most of us had never heard of would bring the entire health, social, economic, political, and business structure to a halt within a few weeks? This health threat has jeopardized our systems across the board. To predict such a calamity, one would have had to be deeply aware of how things interrelate and how every person is connected to every other person on Earth.

Unbeknown to so many people were the facts that we were automating, digitizing, and globalizing almost every aspect of our existence. This unconscious behavior has placed all of us on a vulnerable path. Most individuals or companies have little idea what their digital and cybersecurity risks are, let alone the inadequacies of our public healthcare system to circumvent such a riveting disaster of Biblical proportions.

Yes, the internet and digital systems help with solving so many essential aspects of life and business, but, as we move toward more automation, few of us can understand fully how profound the complexity of the systems we are building are and how fragile and vulnerable they are against traumatic events.[xiv]

This event has had a foundational impact on our operations across the board, causing paradigm shifts so swift that we have all been left in a state of shock. The situation we face is rare, and we must respond by strategizing a wholesale change to our business operations. It is a frightening survival level crisis that we must pivot from toward a new strategy and framework with a creative value system that speaks to the novelty of not only the virus, but of civilization. The COVID-19 virus has been a shock to every company around the world. The pandemic has completely stopped most industries, except food services, healthcare, banking, and communication. Everyone else is on a life raft.

The hope lies in that everyone is not stopped in their tracks and that innovative thinking and great examples of teaming can be found in many sectors of business. I am encouraged by many non-profit startups that are initiating help to our first responders while helping small businesses survive. A great example of this assistance comes from Brooklyn for Life. Started by actor Jeffery Wright, Brooklyn for Life has a twofold objective: to feed the healthcare and frontline first responders and provide revenue for over 40 local restaurants who need help generating income. This creative teaming example is how we must all work together now that we are social distancing and unable to go to businesses in person. This innovative initiative shows how we can create demand and traffic unconventionally and, because it is newsworthy, it has generated authentic content that contemporary viewers are interested in reading and learning. This is an example of how we can approach many business challenges.

I do not believe that we are in the phase of preventing long-lasting COVID-19 business shock as we are in the middle of the first shock waves. There is a warning that this wave could come in three dramatic surges. Will we collapse after each wave or will we work to get ourselves out of shock and into activity, while building the mechanisms necessary to withstand each new wave as it hits? If we do not act decisively, COVID-19 will have long-term effects on our economy and all we will have is the government's sustained measures to give us handouts. We must act quickly because the longer we stay suspended, the harder it will be to break from the yoke of dependence. We have to keep working, even if strategy building is our most proactive response; we can feel hope and progress within this framework. The superheroes are the Jeffery Wrights and Brooklyn for Life projects of this world.

COVID-19 is changing economies, social systems, consumer behaviors, and what customers value and demand. My firm used to work with many retail jewelers and watch companies, and I can assure you that there is little demand for these types of products right now. It used to be that the bridal industry was recession-proof because people still got married even in tough economic times. Now, you cannot have a funeral, let alone a wedding because of the restrictions on social gatherings. Therefore, e-commerce with new tools and techniques for communication and messaging are the new normal and all we have to reflect these novel accommodations. Wedfuly.com is collaborating with Zoom, a video conferencing software, to help couples successfully bring their wedding celebrations online. Bridal companies should initiate integrating with Wedfully and Zoom to be part of the bridal package and create traffic through the resolve of an immediate pain point. We all need love now more than ever, and this is a dynamic way to collaborate with delivering services to the right consumer.

Today's unprecedented unemployment is now even more significant than in the Great Depression; however, people who can continue to work have entirely different motivations. Automation and technology will continue to disrupt and change the playing field. Most companies cannot keep up with the rate of change and worry about life and limb. All of these forces are colliding together at the same time, changing businesses and business systems, such as the supply chain, communication, physical plants, staffing, customer relations, and service. The changes are so swift and the scale so vast that we must accept that most small businesses are in Business SOS™.

Entrepreneurs and CEOs are the first responders when a business is in SOS. Small and large businesses that are not essential are in the tank. Small businesses have more significant credit constraints and are more sensitive to weak consumer demand, so they are often hit the hardest in economic downturns. A subset of small businesses is young businesses that are zero- to five-years-old and are substantial drivers of job creation and productivity growth. Enterprises relying on foot traffic, like restaurants and retail brick and mortar establishments, need to rethink their business model's complete functionality. These types of small businesses have very few employees per establishment, but most employees overall that have been furloughed or let go during the past few months.

As reported by the Brookings Institute's study of small businesses, we see a growing concern for the survival rate of young companies. In that equation are businesses that have novel concepts that must be born during this time period. During the Great Recession, these small businesses experienced disproportionate job loss compared to their share of total employment in the economy. "Nationally, small businesses accounted for 45% of jobs, but, as the economy shed about five million jobs from 2008 to 2009, they accounted for 62% of the net job loss. Compared to the Great Recession, the early stages of the COVID-19 economic crisis suggest that job loss will fall disproportionately within this small business sector."[xv]

Generally, the older and more extensive a small business, the better it fared during the Great Recession. Micro-businesses (fewer than ten employees) and young companies are the most vulnerable across all sectors. The employment losses within these types of companies ranged from 15% in wholesale trades and services to nearly 35% in retail businesses and construction, the latter of which reflects the role housing played in the Great Recession.[xvi]

Restaurants and small retail outlets are likely to lead the losses during these early days of the coronavirus-fueled economic crisis. However, eventually, a significant recession will hit every sector of the small business economy, as consumer demand decreases. This chain reaction will begin first and most intensively with younger and more modest (and, thus, more vulnerable) businesses with larger ones following after. Small companies predominantly serve their local areas, meaning that their viability depends on the health of the critical industries in their local economies. This includes providing all of the necessary safeguards to protect employees and consumers from this pandemic.

The months ahead will be a rollercoaster ride. The outlook for small businesses not in the essential sectors is grim, which is why these precious moments to communicate with big, forward-thinking ideas is paramount to weathering this situation in the long-run. According to a recent McKinsey study on the impact of COVID-19 on businesses: "If the risk of the contagion continues for another 12 to 18 months, public- and private-sector leaders should promote the most effective adaptations and safeguards to economic activity, including physical barriers, face guards, physical distancing, health screenings before entry, and generous and flexible sick leave. Sectors will vary in how critical they are and their ability to safeguard."[xvii]

Rethink Most Social and Economic Systems

In crises, the federal and state governments play essential and expanded roles, protecting people and organizing the response to the crises. However, there will be a power shift to meet the scale and rapid pace of events unfolding during this health crisis. Much of what is compelling is being developed bottom-up. Yes, we can rely on our governors to give us their best efforts. Still, it is up to individual communities to adopt new progressive advances in trial-by-error efforts to jumpstart economies locally, where it matters. This approach will transform long-held expectations about the roles of individuals and institutions.

Defining the Future of Work and Consumption

As discussed in my introduction, the crisis has propelled new technology across all aspects of American life, from e-commerce to remote-working to learning tools, including digital platforms like Venmo, PayPal, Apple, Google Pay, WeChat Work, Zoom, and Google Hangouts. Modern working and shopping practices will probably become permanent fixtures of the next set of technology trends, including digital payments, telehealth, robotics, and entertainment.

Mobilizing Resources with Speed and Scale is Imperative

Within weeks, New York had added tens of thousands of doctors and hospital beds. Several governors invested in new tools to map transmission and rolled out huge economic stimulus plans. Although the central federal government does not have a recently proven ability to mobilize resources in a crisis, we will wait and see if a new vision is on the horizon. The best example is the HIV crisis in the early 1990s in which it was left up to the local governments to develop health strategies. We saw how the central government was slow and late to react in that situation. It appears that the federal response to COVID-19 is running a similar track with no consistent or sustained course but a state to local government initiative.

Non-essential industries, such as entertainment, restaurants, and hotels, are likely to experience adverse shocks on both their supply and demand sides. Many of these industries involve activities that can't be performed at home and, even if they could, consumers seeking to avoid infection are unlikely to demand much of these services. These graphs provided by VOX Research indicate that the magnitude of the shock is considerable, with around a quarter of the economy not functioning.[xviii]

Figure 1 Supply shock factors by occupation

xix

As mentioned in the introduction, when faced with enormous challenges throughout history, man has shown his ability to change and adapt. We have created whole new sectors in the few months that we have been in quarantine only out of sheer necessity. Large companies like Apple, Google, Facebook, and Amazon have the capital to expand their companies into sectors we have not even dreamed of yet. These companies will get larger and become more robust competition for smaller companies. However, an immense opportunity exists for industries to adapt and for new ideas to emerge despite this lack of a level playing field.

Every brick and mortar operation must advance its e-commerce. Everyone is online buying everything from groceries to masks to avoid human contact and practice CDC safety regulations. These companies must invest in the latest e-commerce technology. Real estate is soft, but interest in industrial real estate is on the rise. I have partners in the real estate sector, and their data shows that while homes sales are down in certain regions, consumers are still buying but exclusively through virtual tours and astute lead generating tools. We have needed to reconstitute our supply chain. I don't believe we will rely on offshore production for a while and a resurgence in US manufacturing will be on the rise. There is considerable interest to bring production back to the United States because we were left with embarrassing shortages in vital PPE and consumer goods during the rush to safeguard our hospitals and healthcare workers along with ourselves. Therefore, the need for production, packing, and distribution facilities is on the rise. Large industrial facilities and their works will be in demand for these purposes.

Along with e-commerce is the need to push forward with augmented reality that will enable consumers to see, touch, and feel a product without venturing to a store or showroom. In South Florida, Magic Leap is preparing a full launch of new products for a variety of industries. Out of necessity, we will need robotics and artificial intelligence to safeguard employees from the virus. Students and graduates who are involved with the creation and development of robotics will thrive in the new economy.

With more people on the internet, the advancements in 5G are essential for the growth of many sectors. Education, healthcare, and supply chain all rely on the speed of their connections. The growth of the communication industry and its jobs will be an essential aspect to focus on during these new challenges. We all know that in-person meetings are passé. Virtual meetings have been gobbled up by large companies like Microsoft and Facebook. However, we have seen how small companies are utilizing these

platforms to promote their services, products, and expertise

via these critical platforms.

Freezer and cooler facilities are in demand, which

coincides with the increase in demand related to industrial

real estate. Safely storing food supplies is a must as we

brace the second and third waves of this crisis.

Restaurants that depended on foot traffic are now looking

at take-out as their crucial revenue source and an area of

growth. The rise of Dark Kitchens is a trend, and the need

for quick delivery will increase. As such, food and delivery

services are points of opportunity.

We will see factories spring up closer to distribution points,

and the Walmarts of the world will have to buy American.

The American people were promised more money in our

pockets with free trade; however, the average family has less than $400 saved in case of an emergency. We have been left powerless because of this trickle-down policy. We should not turn our backs on the world, but American-made must be brought back. Manufacturing products on US soil will be the game-changer that will help us recuperate from our devastating losses. We cannot be caught off guard for any necessary products or medicines again. Without policy changes at the central government level to stop outsourcing fundamental supply chain necessities, we will not learn the lessons of our mistakes.

The most critical area of opportunity is education. We now have millions of students from elementary to college, taking online classes and participating in online activities. I believe we will see creative and innovative methods developed by which to teach and engage children and students.

The shock of the shelter-in-place orders and the expedient closing of most businesses to mitigate this virus was catastrophic to our economy. With the stimulus, it seems that Wall Street is functioning and recovering fine. It is Main Street that needs to expedite changes. I am excited and want to affect change one business at a time. Join Business SOS™ and receive help for your business or connect with companies that you feel you can provide support and expertise. We must take up this challenge from the bottom up. Waiting for the central government is not in our cards as a method of survival.

Chapter 2

How Business and Life Has Changed Forever

Where is the New Normal?

With COVID-19 affecting the way we work and live, an immediate need exists for new ways by which collaboration between businesses can be achieved. The process by which to develop new ideas and strategies will also be different in our new work environments as companies and partnerships have to be fundamentally altered. Gone are the days of business meetups in conferences, cafes, or restaurants or a quick discussion over coffee or dinner. Hence, it will be difficult to build personal relationships or personal affinities, which can make conducting business and transactions a little more uncomfortable. Traditional business meetups have been replaced by online video conferences, which will bring about slight differences in the discussion dynamics. Businesses have made significant shifts to accommodate these changes at record speed. They must now make additions to their digital presences so that all aspects of this virtual communication can be seamless. Previously, this could be achieved through phone calls or physical visits to their facilities, which then adds to less productivity. I will outline in this chapter how many of these shifts to online communication will be beneficial for businesses now and in the future. So, it is not all bad news all the time even during COVID-19.

Using online video calls to discuss potential collaborations has multiple benefits. First, significant amounts of time are saved on travel. Second, as the capacity of the meeting is no longer confined to the physical space of the meeting location, the discussion can include many more participants than traditional meetings. This expansion can result in more in-depth reviews taking place with valuable insights being provided from multiple viewpoints. Conducting examinations or liaisons through video calls was once not widely accepted and was regarded as a lazy form of participation. However, COVID-19 has successfully contributed to the shift of video calling becoming a socially acceptable manner of providing input and has significantly changed the general view of online business calls permanently.

Having a more robust online presence for companies means that they can integrate new ideas into their businesses more efficiently. A variety of online tools exist by which to facilitate seamless collaboration through applications, such as Zoom, Google Hangouts, and Google Drive. Many of these tools were previously available, but companies typically stuck with traditional tools, which are slow, inefficient, and obsolete are making the shift to newer collaborative tools. Companies are likely to experience a hike in productivity levels as a positive result.

COVID-19 has necessitated the shift of office work into our homes or to smaller workspaces. Working from home is an idea that has been met with resistance for years, with fears that it would decrease productivity, increase slacking off, and encourage poor focus due to environmental factors. However, this pandemic has shown us that working from home is actually highly viable. Multiple companies have recognized the benefits of working from home and are seriously considering the possibility of a wholesale move of its workforce to the comfort of their individual homes. These companies include Twitter, Morgan Stanley, and Barclays, all of which are titans in their respective fields.

Working from home during COVID-19 can be distracting if you have children or bring about increased productivity and be beneficial for companies' bottom lines. It can certainly help women or men on maternity leave and, during COVID-19, help practice social distancing. Companies have been paying for corporate office space, which can lead to remarkably high costs, primarily if the building is located in a prime business district. These costs can be drastically diminished or even eradicated from the business's operating costs if the company allows its employees to work remotely, which will raise profitability. Time wasted on travelling to and from the office can be saved, reducing staff hours spent in transit. An hour of travelling time each day can quickly add up for each employee, generating massive improvements in moral.

At home, employees can "arrive" to work on time, while not having to get up as early as before due to the lack of travel time necessary. As such, they will be more well-rested and have more energy to put toward their work. With a lack of shared office space, there will be less mini social gatherings or chats, which eat into working hours. Being able to work from home is widely seen as a privilege, as employees can work in the comfort of a familiar environment, which can put them at ease and help them work more effectively. In addition, working at home has proven to be an excellent solution for quarantine and the pandemic thus far. It has brought about some unexpected changes that benefit the employer and employee. Hence, it is likely that the physical office space concept will be entirely revolutionized shortly, with our homes becoming the new offices of tomorrow. We will also see the downsizing of offices space to cut down on overhead.

While this period is an excellent time for businesses to modernize their operations and processes, it is also imperative for companies to realize many new challenges. The most daunting will be if they can survive in this new pandemic age without bringing their businesses and all of their services and selling capabilities online. Almost every restaurant has had to resort to offering take-out or delivery applications to stay in business, as entry to restaurants was prohibited. This must also include a security-based pay-on-line capability. This habit may very well continue long after the lockdown has ended, as people get used to the convenience of delivered food straight to their homes. This type of flexibility and nimbleness is imperative. Businesses that are unable to go online will only be left behind and become obsolete.

The COVID-19 pandemic has also revealed heavy dependencies of businesses on overseas suppliers, which has left them at the mercy of price gouging or a complete lack of supplies, which has drastically affected production. It has signaled to businesses how dangerous being overly reliant on foreign contractors can be. Given the fluid dynamics of world affairs, disasters, such as natural disasters, political conflicts, pandemics, and economic crises, can easily affect other businesses across the world.

Thus, it will benefit companies to either diversify their supply sources or localize their manufacturing and production facilities. This will insulate them from external effects that can often lead to unexpected impacts that will come at a cost. Overseas manufacturing has historically been linked to lower goods and labor costs. Localizing production often results in higher wages and higher product costs. Hence, companies will suffer from a loss in their profit margins. Companies, therefore, have to adapt to the new norm by either engaging in research and development or product differentiation to justify a proportionate increase in their prices to maintain healthy levels of profits.

Current stimulus packages provided by the government have resulted in the wages of workers being thrust into the spotlight. It is unsightly to see how unemployment payments can often be higher than the workers' current wages. Simply stated, revealing that workers are being paid too little or there is not enough margin for owners to pay more. This means that businesses will have to find ways to improve their workforce usage through enhanced technology and training, which will likely create an upward increase in workers' wages as they are likely to begin demanding higher salaries due to newly acquired and valued skills. Businesses will, thus, have to keep up with output to maintain profitability.

Stimulus payments have also resulted in massive amounts of money being used by the government to keep the economy afloat. These funds will likely translate to higher taxes being imposed on businesses and individuals in the future. Companies can lose profitability due to increased taxes, or they must find ways to improve their profitability to combat the rise in taxes. Many of the methods by which companies can drive profitability start with developing multiple revenue streams. Large mature brands have practiced these brand extensions for years. It is time for small companies to see the benefits of developing multiple revenue streams within one product or service capability.

As people are stuck at home and will remain so in the near future, spending on online goods has increased. E-commerce giant Shopify reported revenues of $470 million in the first quarter of 2020, which was a 47% increase from the previous year. Much of this increase has been attributed to salaries being spent online rather than at the usual entertainment venues, such as bars, pubs, cinemas, and amusement parks.[xx]

The potential of online sales is staggering, and it can be expected for businesses to bring their full scope of operations online or new companies to take advantage of this new spending habit. The competition will be rough, and businesses may still find themselves at a disadvantage when attempting to retool their products and service offerings online. Over-riding demand exists that many small businesses do not know or understand the complexities of creating sufficient engagement and online marketing.

Online marketing is a growing industry, with it taking up more of a market share than traditional advertising avenues, such as television and billboards, annually. More businesses are becoming inclined to advertise online as people are spending more time on their phones, tablets, and computers. Valuable ad space offered by social media giants, such as Instagram, Facebook, and YouTube, is expected to generate $336 billion in revenue in 2020.[xxi]

Online advertising has become extremely sophisticated, with tools available that can target niche audiences. Lead generating software and expertise is paramount when attempting to adjust to social distancing. The traditional sales call is obsolete. It will be the inbound traffic that will define a company. Finding and communicating with new markets is the only way to scale faster.

Everything will now be virtual. Hiring will not be an in-person interview, but a virtual call. With this new complexity of needs and given the current climate, it has become challenging to hire through the usual processes. Instead, companies are opting to hire contractors that have heavily specialized skills. The rise in demand for contractors or freelancers has led to sites, such as Fiverr, Upwork, and Bark. These sites allow for freelancers to offer their specialized services for a more reasonable fee. Customers can seek help with a limitless number of tasks in things like video editing, logo design, setting up email blasts, developing video advertisements, or even finding help in setting up new e-commerce stores on Amazon or Walmart.

The new thrust of online production will lead to unprecedented remote hiring of talent and will drive up the prices of these services, which can lead to positive results for both the customer and companies. Contractors who once operated exclusively for major companies will be attracted to join the freelance industry due to the ability to charge high fees. Smaller companies will also be able to gain access to top-quality contractors who were previously not in the market. This change will allow companies to find the best workers, which will help their businesses grow with controlled overhead, unlike before.[xxii]

The recent pandemic has left many businesses bankrupt or on the verge. These companies previously reported enormous profits, but have spent almost every cent on expansions that could not weather the business downturn brought about by the pandemic. It is becoming increasingly apparent that businesses will have to learn to set aside sufficient cash to allow for company sustainability during this or any crisis. This will likely result in slower growth in markets in the future. Despite all of it, this growth during the pandemic will allow for much more stability and sustainability than ever before. Stronger and more resilient businesses will be built out of this pandemic. Companies that were financially prudent before will be heavily rewarded as competitors find themselves unable to survive in the current economic downturn. As I complete this chapter, businesses are beginning to reopen with much trepidation. The stock market is up, but Main Street is on life support. Small companies have no choice, but to try to begin even under the direst of circumstances. Now there are protests in the streets begging for reform of police departments. None of this will increase consumer confidence or drive a strong economy. However, this is now who we are! We have problems, serious problems, but we must figure out how to thrive even in tough economic times because there does not seem to be any time soon when it will change. It is time to adapt to life in this new economy and still "bring home the bacon." I have full confidence that there is a way.

Chapter 3

Partnerships and Integration

A Collective Big Think!

What are the big ideas that will frame all strategic and organizational changes to come for small businesses? We know, from American history, that big ideas emerge from crises. The most important task right now is to strategize what will work in, first, the short- and, then, the long-term. The main issue will be deciding what the new supply and demand needs are now and what will be important for future scale. Most entrepreneurs have a secret vision of what new products and services will be requested post-pandemic. Life has changed forever, and it is critical that we don't go back, but move forward. "We can't go back to the way we were. Instead, we must become a more adaptable, learning organization, competing not only with scale, but also speed. We must rediscover business building—to disrupt the status quo and step confidently from this crisis into a much-changed, new world." In his book, Bernd Schmitt notes the irony that many business leaders and their organizations want big thinking, "but cannot produce it because their organizations are trapped in a mode of small thinking that kills creativity right from the start. This kind of 'Small Think' is characterized by inertia and resistance, narrow-mindedness, and risk aversion that stifle true innovation." Larger organizations will notice this in their functional silos that behave independently. "Small Think is what managers get paid to do."[xxiii]

By thinking big and formulating a collaborative effort to redesign our small businesses one company and community at a time, groups of companies can then pull themselves from survival mode—or worse, the magical moment of reinvention. Good leaders and their companies can make more connections, see a greater purpose, and move to a new kind of COVID-19 normalcy. Not only does this rejuvenate the sheer joy of running a business, but, we can also, through our networks restore and reconstitute our businesses. Many have intuitively been adapting to this type of horizontal business model out of necessity.

Forms of Alignment

Once the "Big Think" dawns, leaders have three basic options: they can build the expertise, machinery, and/or capacity needed; they can buy it (i.e., outsource it); or they can ally themselves with other companies. This alliance can take one of three basic forms: a strategic alliance, a joint venture, or a consortium. Legally, these forms are beyond this book's scope. This chapter focuses on allying with other companies in some sort of partnership, meaning any of the three forms of alliance.

Each day we are asked to provide faster and more efficient services and product delivery in the middle of a pandemic. How can we possibly meet the demand before it is too late if we do not align with or trust in colleagues to help guide us so that we gain traction? I have read countless articles about partnerships. Yet, many of us simply do not have the confidence, knowledge, or skills necessary to find and forge profitable and non-litigious relationships at the speed that would be necessary in these troublesome times. Many of us simply have not developed this level of what I call "IT liquidity" or the complex network of relationships that make working with new, unknown partners an easy model to follow.

Business SOS™ will provide, through its website and membership, the ability to connect to a specific source, vendor, alliance, or partner with the desirable assets to reinvigorate a business. We will also utilize a membership agreement for this service. It is based on a commitment to establish the highest level of corporate governess and business ethics—values that should always be part of our American culture. I think it necessary to reestablish this in order to revivify our diminishing corporate culture. Our community is in crisis, and each member needs to provide the leadership and opportunities to trust others. By utilizing the Business SOS™ infrastructure, individual companies will be allowed the resources to support one another in this community-based effort. In summary, we need to trust each other to create the level of change we need at the fast pace we need it without looking over our shoulders.

Partnerships

Most companies are unable to house all of their disciplines and resources, human or otherwise, in a single infrastructure. In our current climate, the primary reasons are financially and competency-driven. We simply do not have enough capital to develop our businesses or manage the rapid advances in technology as in the past when business strategies were developed vertically.

My agency houses all of the disciplines under one roof: strategic thinking, account service, creative direction, production, media buying, public relations, traffic, copywriting, webmasters, and digital strategy experts. Today, I would not think of developing an infrastructure that large because of the overhead costs as well as the inefficient and slow rate of service delivery. IT now provides the ability to function with employees and executives working through cloud computing in one office or many locations. This new virtual office structure has proven that it works and that executives and line staff can be even more productive than in traditional settings. This is another example of how drastic IT has changed in regard to how business services are managed and delivered.[xxiv] This flexibility is a positive outcome, but, with these new advantages, the customer becomes increasingly demanding in his/her expectations. The result is adopting a 24/7 availability of secure and top quality, client service 365 days a year from day one. I have found that there are thousands of digital agencies, but few that can deliver the quality of creative and technological skills required to keep pace with this changing environment. This is very important because the internet is unforgiving when it comes to speed and service. Wolfgang Feisst, an executive of SAP, stated: "Today, we deliver a service that needs to run the first time on. That means that every hour, day-by-day, we are faced with customer needs, and it means each vendor needs to deliver a high level of service."[xxv]

These changes and investments are the types that most small businesses find daunting. Cloud computing, although offering a do-it-yourself capacity for business owners, results in many owners having to manage a more complex, hybrid environment. Once this environment was inside the company, but, now, it's outside the firm. Many times, small businesses do not have the depth of understanding of needs related to Cloud or the resources to create the multiple accounts necessary for the various aspects of their business.

The skill to utilize Cloud services is the leap that so many of us are afraid to take. Most small business owners are control-oriented. Changing this strategy keeps costs down and communication up, but requires a level of trust from business owners in these exterior source providers. By using Business SOS™ and its committed culture of honesty and corporate governess, business owners will be able to create easy partnerships or alliances to acquire business capacities their business may be too small by themselves to handle or expand their market reach into broader, possibly even global, trading areas. IT and cloud computing are intuitively fostering professionals seeking quid-pro-quo relationships. Business SOS™ will be the training ground.[xxvi]

How will this network work? Business SOS™ website members will complete a questionnaire that documents their businesses. The answers will record, bit-by-bit, the complete DNA of each company. Again, these companies will range from concept to currently distressed status. So, different types of information need to be collected from the rationale behind the name and its digital significance to the date of incorporation and the financial life cycle of the business to the products and services provided to whether the business model is still viable during and post-COVID-19 to what resources are needed by the business to get it out of survival mode and back on track. Each resource company is guided by its commitment to work with the highest level of ethics and corporate governess because many of our businesses and business owners are in a vulnerable state of distress. They need a significant level of comfort and reassurance when discussing the intimate details of their businesses.

Partnerships and alliances with key people and companies are crucial for small businesses to succeed. Good alliances help businesses overcome tumultuous financial and socially stressful times. The key objectives of strategic business alliances are:

1. Innovating products and/or services for the post-COVID-19 world

2. Entering new markets and/or reaching new customers

3. Increasing production and delivery capacity, while keeping inventory lean

4. Ensuring a least expensive supply of raw materials and/or resources

5. Increasing market share and/or outrunning competitors

6. Improving after-sale customer service

Strategic alliances can help companies provide security, software, technology, service, and consultation. The number of solid alliances they develop and maintain affects their growth phase post-COVID-19.[xxvii]

How to Set Up a Strategic Alliance

Strategic alliances are sweeping through nearly every industry and becoming an essential driver of potential growth. Alliances range in scope from informal business relationships based on simple contracts to joint venture agreements in which, for legal and tax purposes, either corporations or partnerships are set up to manage the alliances.

For small businesses, strategic alliances are a way to work with others toward a common goal, while not losing their individuality. Alliances are a way of reaping the rewards of a team effort—and the gains from forming strategic alliances appear to be substantial. Companies participating in alliances report that as much as 18% of their revenues come from their alliances. However, it isn't just profit that is motivating this increase in alliances. Other factors include an increasing intensity of competition, a growing need to operate on a glo-cal scale, a fast-changing marketplace, and industry convergence in many markets (i.e., the synergy between service and manufacturing companies are increasingly overlapping in the products/services they supply). Especially in a time when marketing must be part of product development and is becoming the norm, these partnerships can leverage a

company's growth through alliances with international

partners. Business SOS™ is here to make these transitions

more automated and readily available to its members so

that they do not have to take on unnecessary risks and

expenses.

A *strategic alliance* is essentially a partnership in which

you combine efforts in projects ranging from getting a

better price for supplies by buying in bulk together to

building a product with each company providing part of its

production. The goal of alliances is to minimize risk while

maximizing leverage and profit.

Alliances are often confused with mergers, acquisitions,

and outsourcing. While there are similarities in the

circumstances in which a business might consider one of

these solutions, they are far from the same. Mergers and

acquisitions are permanent, structural changes in how the company exists. Outsourcing is simply a way of purchasing a functional service for the company.

An *alliance* is simply a business-to-business collaboration. Another phrase that is frequently used in conjunction with alliances is establishing a business network. Alliances are formed for joint marketing, joint sales or distribution, joint production, design collaboration, technology licensing, and research and development. Relationships can be vertical between a vendor and a customer or horizontal between vendors—local or global. In order to rapidly react to the current business climate and assist our companies, we will activate every potential source relationship for our members. The results will be:

- The achievement in advantages of scale, scope, and speed;
- Increased market penetration;
- Enhanced competitiveness in domestic and/or global markets;
- Enhanced product development;
- The develop of new business opportunities through new products and services;
- Expansion related to market development;
- Increased exports;
- Diversification;
- The creation of new businesses; and
- A reduction in costs.

Strategic alliances are becoming an increasingly common tool for expanding the reach of companies without committing to expensive internal expansions beyond the companies' core businesses. We need to help each other develop the skill sets necessary to make team or business alliances work quickly and easily.[xxviii]

Growth of "Teaming"

From the football field to the boardroom, a coordinated team effort is critical. The drive toward product or service differentiation has led firms to concentrate on niche markets and provide highly specialized services and products. In addition, competition has fostered outsourcing of all, but the core capabilities of a firm. In this environment, *teaming*—firms seeking partners to provide commodities and services as needed. The growth in the size and complexity of our business environments has resulted in the necessity of a team effort.

Government Teaming

Remember the Department of Defense (DOD) Guidebook I discussed in my last book. Its purpose was to assist small firms in successfully bidding on larger defense projects. It provided acquisition strategy teams with a road map on how a group of small businesses could meet the requirements. Although this strategy alone will not overcome every problem faced by small businesses, it does open the door by broadening competition on large DOD contracts. The guidebook also serves as a resource for acquisition strategy teams to help level the playing field for small businesses. It offers several examples of real-world strategies that can be used to encourage the participation of teams in DOD acquisitions.[xxix]

Even the language sounded familiar to that used by our initial strategy members. So, the government is well-aware that a level playing field does not exist small businesses whether they are looking to bid on a government contract or are competing with Wal-Mart in a local market. The acknowledgement confirms that a problem exists for which they are trying to find a solution through the Small Business Administration. We need the government at all levels to help small businesses develop these teaming skills and initiatives. It does not have to be a strategy secretly utilized only for defense contracts, but could also be an all-out effort to help bring small businesses out of survival mode and foster global business outreach of these businesses, increasing our exports and initiating U.S. leadership in global expansion post-COVID-19.[xxx]

Teaming Pros and Cons

Although teaming is a customary business strategy for most large businesses, many small firms often practice a go-it-alone strategy for a variety of reasons. For example, some small business owners do not want to give up control. Others avoid teaming because they want to have direct relationships with their customers, and teaming (as a subcontractor) may mean either no relationship or minimal contact with the main customers. Still, others fear to invest

in a proposal, only to be squeezed out by the prime

contractor, who refuses to negotiate with a team member.

Additional reasons include limited resources (e.g., legal

expertise) or prior negative teaming experiences.

Mergers and Acquisitions 3.0

Mergers and acquisitions (M&A) are other tools for re-

establishing business and your business skillset. An

acquisition is when one company absorbs another, usually

through some combination of cash and stock and assumes

all the assets and liabilities of the acquired firm. A *merger,*

in contrast, is when two firms are worth more together than

they were apart. By joining forces, they could start a

positive financial strategy and experience a quick

turnaround for growth and profitability. Either approach

could speed up the growth process for many small

businesses that do not have the time to do market research

and lay the groundwork for expanding in new or global markets. Matching firms that would benefit from an M&A takes patience and trust.

At Business SOS™, our teams will watch for these prime growth opportunities for companies to join forces. Along with providing critical speed to the growth process, an M&A is a great strategy by which to assemble the kind of talent necessary to meet a larger market's demand. Most owners seek out the sort of company management to expand their businesses. If talent is promoted to stay on after the M&A, it also allows companies to buy knowledge that sometimes takes years to acquire.

M&As are another way by which to enter new markets in a connected world. To think and grow in this new business climate, we have to adapt to a new way of thinking about our business models and life cycles. It is no longer about creating a company and expecting that company to function the same in the next year as it did in the previous two years. We need to erase our boundaries and borders and collaborate at a more rapid pace to join forces with our business colleagues.

Business SOS™ wants to create a culture in which competitors need not be bitter rivals, but view each other as possible collaborators at the right moment of growth or stagnation. This is what our large business counterparts have known and done for years. M&As can and will be part of the solution for many of our struggling companies. For example, picture a business that has been in survival mode for four years. This strategy could realize economic gains, such as economies of scale, combining complementary resources, garnering tax advantages, and eliminating inefficiencies. Other reasons for considering growth through an acquisition include property rights to products or services, increasing market power and brand awareness, penetrating new geographic regions, and providing management with new opportunities for growth and advancement at a faster pace.

"In today's glo-cal business environment, companies may have to grow to survive, and one of the best ways to grow is by merging with another company or acquiring other companies," said business consultant Jaclyn Sherriton in an interview with *Entrepreneur Magazine*. "Massive multi-billion-dollar corporations are becoming the norm, leaving an entrepreneur to wonder whether a merger ought to be in his or her plans as well," Sherriton continued.[xxxi]

Without solid ethical resources in M&As, Business SOS™ would not have a complete complement of offerings to the post-COVID-19 entrepreneur. We need to make these resources easily evaluated by our members, affordable, and delivered by a group of ethical volunteers and professionals.

Promoting and providing the entire suite of offerings to businesses, which includes partnerships, alliances, teaming, and mergers will afford many small businesses the opportunity to survive and thrive in these continued dysfunctional economic times.

Chapter 4

Our New Business Environment

Sweatpants Executives

Smaller Offices, Home Office and Remote Work. It Works!

Like many entrepreneurs, I started in my living room. This location worked until I realized that I needed a stage and a professional place to grow. For a woman in the early 90s in the last century, this was of the utmost importance as you would not invite a male executive to your home/office. At that time, I bought a Louis 16th secretary table from a famous woman in the real estate business, Casey Cousins. She had made millions working at that desk and later sold her company, Cousins and Associates, to Merrill Lynch. Her success was inspirational to me as a young entrepreneur. Not long ago, she told me to make a beautiful conference room, get a good maid, and serve an elegant lunch instead of fighting over the check at lunch with a male executive. Such an action would show them you are in control but still keep your femininity and power. I am not sure we have evolved much more as most key executives in A suites are still men, and, if they are women, we are still fighting for equal pay. However, that was the recommended optimal work environment when I started with an office receptionist/assistant and production staff. I will tell you that her advice did allow me to command my stage, which provided me with the power I needed to grow my business larger than some of my male counterparts. That was a traditional work environment for the times. Then companies like WeWork and Regus evolved into coworking environments. These coworking environments sprang up in the first part of the 21st century to accommodate new startups or smaller companies that needed to save on overhead expenses and utilize the networking opportunities that coworking environments facilitated.

Since COVID-19, the majority of us have had to stay at home and work remotely, and the entire business environment is in flux. Coworking office spaces no longer work, and they will not work for quite a while because experts say that we will not have a vaccine or remedy, nor do the experts expect one until next year. Sitting in close proximity to other workers is simply not safe. I have spoken with a variety of business owners, and they simply don't want to spend the overhead costs necessary to maintain and renew lease agreements when we can have a second or third wave of COVID-19 and forced home again.

Office liability does not bode well for the commercial real estate sector. Major metropolitan areas like New York, Chicago, and Los Angeles, and major financial institutions and larger companies will segment and hire workers with these considerations of at least 30% of workers working from home. Owners must understand that, even though this structural work environmental change has occurred rapidly and without warning, these changes will be long-lasting and will affect the internal environment of businesses now and post COVID-19.

The current overriding safety issue will affect day-to-day decisions for the next two years. Generally, we choose the supplies we purchase, which employees to hire, the products to sell, and where we sell those products. For each business today, and any new startups, these decision-making processes will experience quantum changes to the physical plant to the legal issues that govern each company or office environment. Right now, Congress wants to enact a law that companies, like meat processing plants, cannot be sued because the president has called them all back to work so that we do not suffer shortages during the COVID-19 quarantine and forward. Democrats want specific sunset clauses, or line item clauses that do not allow workers to be at- risk from injury after the pandemic comes to a close— leaving workers without the safeguards of the legal obligation of company owners to adhere to safe working conditions and environments.

However, the external environmental conditions, such as a national health crisis or banking failures, that affect your businesses are generally beyond the control of owners, and these changes are drastic. Business owners and managers must be vigilant and continuously study the environment so that they can adapt their businesses accordingly. The natural disaster of this pandemic will have a significant impact on internal environmental structures and external conditions. A complete re-evaluation of the external environment that will make products and services timely or obsolete. We now see more than ever that health issues, such as a highly transmitted virus, can cause a complete economic, social, and environmental breakdown of all of our businesses. If not mitigated, we have warning by the experts the virus can run out of control and completely overwhelm our hospital systems across the country and the world. We are now in different phases of reopening and may need to lockdown again because of high case counts. States are attempting a reopen through the summer of 2020, hoping they will not see a new wave in the fall. As we slowly begin opening, we become aware that all aspects of our businesses have changed or reprioritized. Now more than ever, the acceleration of automation and technology matters more. Our past ways of communicating need a complete revision.

The entire myriad of social factors such as our attitudes, values, ethics, and lifestyles influence what, how, where, and when people purchase products and services. All of these mitigating factors are going through drastic changes.

Many businesses are going through a quantum thrashing, not just travel, and restaurants, but all business models. It will not be obvious to predict which companies and products will survive, but we need to define and measure relevance in this new environment. People of all ages will have a broader range of interests vastly different from their pre-COVID-19 consumer profiles. Changing roles have brought more women entrepreneurs to become the fastest growing sector of new business development. This new development will help stabilize or increase family incomes, heighten demand for time-saving goods and services, change family shopping patterns, and impact individuals' ability to achieve a work-life balance. At the same time, we have to blur the lines between work time at home or home office. I believe we must always focus on American ethics and values with a renewed emphasis within organizations and at all levels of the company. Owners and employees are searching for the right approach when it comes to gender and even age inequality, and other social behaviors that impact the potential for a business's continued success. The dress code will also change, and the advent of the sweatpants executives may be more far-reaching than just single proprietors in the gig economy.

With so many employees trusted to work at home, we will see vast differences in what workers purchase for business wear. Addressed in a recent article in The Atlantic by Amanda Mulls, we find that "Millennials, notorious murderers of American institutions and social norms, are now the largest generation in the country's workforce. As the oldest members of that group, people in their late 30s, accrue power in their organizations, they've started to reshape the meaning of '"work clothes"' in their image— upending the very idea of a dress code as a single standard to which all should aspire. When they're done, work clothes might be dead for good. Whether that future looks like a descent into midriff-baring anarchy or a sweet reprieve from the tyranny of binding waistbands probably depends on whether you're a person who makes rules or one who is subject to them."[xxxii]

The standard for professional office wear has long been a suit or a conservatively tailored dress. I do not think this applies to workers who don't go into an office any longer. However, this style of dress has primarily held up the standard despite the successful invasion of "business casual," started by most designer brands like J. Crew, Brooks Brothers, and Men's Warehouse, and more. Many of the world's largest businesses, like Google, Twitter, Facebook, and Apple, and non-tech companies allowed their employees to come to work in jeans and sweatshirts all week have yet to destabilize the work environment and their employees' productivity. Throughout my career, I have believed that one must dress appropriately to be taken seriously. That meant a suit and tie for a man and a skirt and jacket for a woman. I will date myself now as I believe even today to be taken seriously; one must dress in a suit for men that means with a tie and for women that means skirt and jacket. Just before COVID-19, I would walk into a meeting only to be met with casually dressed CTOs, and clients would not blink. Nor should they. This behavior revivifies this new change to sweatpants executives as an ongoing trend because the traditional ques of credibility are less in the manner of your dress and more in how cool you look. Fashion expert Juan Salazar, known for restyling many high powered as well as newbie executives for the current work environments says; "this is a moment to carve a unique individual style for work at home wardrobes. I still have clients who need to be presentable on Zoom indicating that fashion will reemerge but many designers won't survive." This shedding of companies will give new young designers a chance to capture the moment with comfortable and wearable collections. Returning to suites, ties and skirts just may not connote preparedness and success and date the executive as living in the past or BC era (Before COVID).

There is a sea change between our internalized notions about professionalism and what a company's dress code says, which is why the traditional ques and guardrails must be replaced with something that sends a professional message, even if the clothing is not formal but more casual. The first impression of competence based on traditional dress has been so durable, in part, because for years, the mass media have told us that A suite executives wear well-cut suits or formal sheath dresses in neutral tones.

According to Ms. Mull, who says, "Had our first glimpses of *Mad Men's* Don Draper or *Scandal's* Olivia Pope caught them in cutoffs and a raggedy souvenir T-shirt from spring break, their world-beating dominance might not have been as evident. In a twist in the we-are-what-we-wear story, researchers at Harvard identified what they called the red-sneakers effect. It posits that as long as the person ignoring workplace guidelines is perceived to be doing it purposefully, the dominance of that person improves— think Mark Zuckerberg and his" 'f**k you'" hoodies in early Facebook business meetings." After all, their higher power than is being exempt from the rules that govern everyone else."[xxxiii]

The external business environment today during and after COVID-19 will be much more complicated than your office size or the manner of your dress. It will include the complexities of economic, political, and legal, demographic, social, competitive, local, global, and technological trends and movements. Instead of fear, we must embrace how the external environment is changing and assess the impact of those changes on every business and business model.

Based on historical trends, we believe that those individuals working remotely before the pandemic will continue to work remotely, even after the pandemic is over. Increasing this remote trend even after they are allowed to return to their offices. We believe that there will be a significant upswing in the adoption of remote work. Our best estimate is that we will see 25%-30% of the workforce working from home on the multiple -days- of the week by the end of 2021 for several reasons.[xxxiv]

First, the demand for flexibility related to where and how people work has been building for decades. Before the crisis, surveys repeatedly showed that 80% of employees wanted to work from home at least some of the time. Over a third stated that they would take a pay cut in exchange for the option. While the experience of working at home during the crisis may not have been ideal as whole families sheltered in place, it has given people a taste of what it is like, and many individuals, like myself, like it a lot and get more done. The genie is out of the bottle, and it's not likely to go back in. One of the biggest holdbacks of remote work is trust—managers simply don't trust their people to work untethered. They're used to managing by counting butts- in-seats, rather than by results. That's not managing, that's baby-sitting. What's more, seeing the back of someone's head tells an owner nothing about whether that person is actually working. When business owners ask, "How will I know if they're working?" I ask, "How do you know they are working now?"[xxxv]

Because of this rapid change, management needs to change its processes to be focused on results and productivity.

Micromanagement doesn't work, and neither does "managing by walking around". If people are forced to work at home for an extended period, as it appears, they will be, owners will have to learn to hire better and trust their employees more.

Second, the inefficient way that we utilize office space is worth going forward. One of the reasons that climate change experts have a hard time getting people to change their habits is that the impact is hard to see. In the early days of the global response to COVID-19, we are starting to see a dramatic reduction in traffic, congestion, and pollution. While, sadly, sustainability has not been a primary driver of remote work in recent years, being able to actually see the difference it can make may finally flip the switch for employers and employees. According to a recent article in Forbes, the annual environmental impact of working remotely half of the time would be the greenhouse gas equivalent of taking the entire New York State workforce off the road. There is no easier, quicker, and cheaper way by which to reduce your carbon footprint than by reducing commuter travel.[xxxvi]

Third, COVID-19 will also likely cause executives to rethink the need for travel to meetings and, conferences and training. They will learn that, while virtual meetings may not have all the same benefits of being face-to-face, the savings may outweigh the costs most of the time. For most small businesses, the savings may make the difference between staying solvent or going broke. A typical employer can save about $11,000/a year for every person who works remotely half of the time. These same employees can save between $2,500 and $4,000 a year (working remotely half the time) and even more if they can move to a less expensive area and work remotely full time.

We are now hyper-aware of health risks, whether real or imagined and employers are hypersensitive about the potential for liability if people get sick at work. It is a benefit of the digital age to be able to work out home and social distance.

During this pandemic, I have asked myself why we have not been as vigilant before this pandemic, especially during flu season. It is standard that, when one person gets the flu, everyone gets the flu shortly after. It would have been unheard of to ask that person to wear a mask and take his/her temperature. These gestures would have been a privacy infringement. From now on during flu season, we should protect each other by wearing a mask.

When we return to offices regularly, there will need to be strict protocols for each sector. We will need to be able to enforce restrictions and provide appropriate supplies.

For onsite workers, there will need to be giant sanitizing stations and plenty of extra cleaners available to all employees. There are even thermal scanners that will need to be installed that will beep if someone has a temperature. The office manager or operations officers will have to take on the responsibility of assessing whether a staff member looks sick and should be sent home. Other safeguards could include a sneeze guard, which is a low cost but helps separate receptionists and workers from colleagues' aerosols germs. We may have to stagger our workforces if there is not enough room available for social distancing. "Organizations will need to working out who most needs to be at the office, and capping staff numbers off at about 30%, which is probably the sweet spot for social distancing," says De Plazaola. For starters, he foresees firms subsidizing home offices, given that the home is now considered a legitimate workspace.[xxxvii]

A shift to home working could "liberate" parts of the workforce, such as working mothers and those employees who live far from major cities and have struggled to find work. I have always worked in the creative services business. Coming together for a great brainstorming session has always been a highlight of our creative process. In the advertising and marketing business, it has facilitated great collaborations and the coming together of good ideas and concepts to find the right marketing for a client. Yes, most people work to earn money, but we also work because we enjoy coming together to create ideas and solve problems. I think that's what we've been missing these past few weeks. That sense of connection is fundamental to the human race.

In the longer term, experts predict that society's heightened awareness of contagious diseases could usher in a new type of office – one that has elements in common with a hospital. We are approaching challenging economic times, and few small businesses will have the budgets to retro-fit each office. However, they can add more regular disinfecting cleanings with possible ultra-violet lights or better air filtration systems or filter changes. Handshakes have already become obsolete, but hand washing should become a ritual with a small squirt of hand sanitizer every time we meet.

Already elevators are becoming touchless, and, soon, there will be apps to make sure all aspects of opening and closing are touchless. For example, employees could eliminate the need to press communal buttons using their smartphone to send a command to the elevator or staff coffee machine. Conference rooms could be fitted out with voice-activated technologies to control lighting, audio, and visual equipment. Passing through doors or flushing the toilet would require a simple wave, while self-service in office kitchens could become a relic of the past, to be replaced with automation or a dedicated server.[xxxviii]

The external financial environment is quite grim. That is why I want to be proactive for all small businesses with relevant business models. We have not seen such a rise in unemployment since the Great Depression. There are all kinds of economic storms on the horizon if we do not get our act together. Once a company is stalled because of COVID-19, it will take a lot of capital and effort to reconstitute many of these businesses. Economic influence is one of the most important external forces on markets. Fluctuations in the levels of economic activity create business cycles that affect companies and individuals in many ways. When the economy is stalled or stopped, as in the case of the first and second quarters of 2020, unemployment rates are high, and income levels fall dramatically. Inflation and interest rates are other areas that change according to economic activity and are, currently, relatively low. Government, through the policies it sets with tax and interest rates, will attempt to stimulate or curtail the level of economic activity. Besides, supply and demand forces determine how prices and quantities of goods and services behave in a free market. Right now, demand is high in sectors like food, food services, and healthcare. Most other industries are just beginning to reopen.

The political climate of a country is another critical factor for business owners to consider in their day-to-day business operations when reopening. The amount of government activity, the types of laws it passes, and the general political stability of a government are three components of the political climate. For example, a multinational company, such as Monsanto, will evaluate the political climate of our country and other foreign countries before deciding to close or open plants in the U.S. once more.[xxxix]

We are hoping that a careful balance in bringing back manufacturing to America is met with the need to maintain a global presence of American goods and services. How restrictive regulations are for businesses, and whether any new policies will address climate change that will affect businesses and business development. Import tariffs, quotas, and export restrictions also must be taken into account.

Demographic factors are uncontrollable factors in the business environment and are extremely important to business owners. Demography is the study of people's vital statistics, such as age, gender, race, and ethnicity, and location. Demographics help companies define the markets for their products and determine their workforce's' size and composition. Demographics are at the heart of many business decisions. Businesses today must deal with the wholly altered shopping preferences of different generations, each requiring different marketing approaches and goods and services targeted to their needs.

The application of technology will be the catalyst to stimulate growth in the U.S. or any other economic system. Technology is the application of science and engineering skills and knowledge to solve production and organizational problems, which will matter more now than ever. New equipment, software, robots, and other automation that improve productivity and reduce costs will be among a company's most valuable assets. Productivity is the number of goods and services one worker can produce. Our ability as a nation to maintain and build wealth depends, in a large part, on the speed and effectiveness with which we use technology— to invent and adopt more efficient equipment to improve manufacturing productivity, to develop new products, and to process information so that it can be made instantly available across the organization and to suppliers and customers. Many U.S. businesses, large and small, use technology to create change, improve efficiencies, and streamline operations.[xl]

However, many are still not utilizing the vast resources that technology can provide. For example, advances in cloud computing allow businesses to access and store data without running applications or programs housed on physical computers or servers in their offices. Such applications and programs can now be accessed through the internet. Mobile technology allows businesses to communicate with employees, customers, suppliers, and others at the swipe of a tablet or smartphone screen. Robots help companies to automate repetitive tasks that free up workers to focus on more knowledge-based tasks critical to business operations. For each company, you need to evaluate if you will continue being sweatpants executives or reconstitute your office space to be more in keeping with current healthcare necessities. Each company will be tasked to look at their environments to evaluate the following:

1. Define the components of your internal and external business environments.

2. What factors within the current economic environment affect your businesses?

3. What demographic shifts and technological developments create both challenges and new opportunities for your business?

The coronavirus pandemic will have a lasting effect on the habits and customs of our society. The workplace has suffered the most disruption. Many of us working at home had to go through several tough weeks trying to establish some sense of normalcy while juggling children in virtual

classrooms and spouses or partners dealing with office

setups and I.T. efficiencies. With all of us at home, what do

our work hours look like? 9-5? or is it 5-7 and then

childcare and breakfast and then go to 6? They say work

hours at home have grown by as much as 20%. Perhaps

unsurprisingly, their data has also revealed that digital

collaborations are growing, in the public sector, where

cooperation has risen by 142%. This digital workflow has

seen growth in the number of apps we're using, including

services for videoconferencing, chat and messaging, cloud

storage and sharing tools.[xli]

It is a real-life human tragedy we have been hit by a once in

a century pandemic just a little over a decade after the

Great Recession. This dramatic event will cause massive

changes in our internal and external business environments.

It will have serious economic indications for all of us. Yet, amid the tragedy and uncertainty runs a strong undercurrent of hope. Individuals and communities have responded with empathy and strength. Organizations, despite many staring down the barrel of layoffs, furloughs, and shutdowns, took fast action to protect their workers' health and safety, establish essential services, and deploy workforce strategies to support workers in real-time. An ecosystem banded together to leverage their collective and complementary capabilities to effect meaningful change. The most significant change will be technological changes hitting small businesses like yet another avalanche of challenges. So, the fortitude of the entrepreneur will be tested once again. I am hoping that, through Business SOS™, we can make these changes bittersweet.

Since 2008, we have seen the speed and scale of change continue to accelerate, with technological advances bringing bigger and bolder moves in a shorter window of time. However, as new technologies and digital transformations dominated conversations in boardrooms, human concerns were considered separate from, if not directly in conflict with, technological advances.

COVID-19 has reinforced our conviction that human concerns are not separate from technological advances, but integral for organizations looking to capture the full value of the technologies that are mandatory to survive and scale any business. As organizations looked to adapt their ways of working in response to the crisis, they will find that technology will be the biggest hurdle because of the speed of change. We will be forced to create new habits and management practices related to how people adapt, behave, and work in partnership with the technology available to them; to fulfil distinctly human needs, such as the desire for meaning, connection, and well-being at work; to maximize worker potential through the cultivation of capabilities and to safeguard ethical values.[xlii]

This crisis presents a unique opportunity for organizations that can overcome the instinct of treating humans and machines on parallel paths to build instead connections that can pave a way forward, nurturing growth and innovation in the weeks, months, and years to come. It also serves as a window into what can happen if the intersections of humanity and, technology, and the opportunity to operate as an actual social enterprise are not fully embraced. In light of COVID-19, the chance (and risk) may never be more significant for organizations to transcend this paradox and see a possibility.

COVID-19 has challenged business leaders to do three things: stage the return to work, understand and leverage the advancements they enacted during the crisis, and chart a new path forward. Focusing on the back to work process

alone is not a viable option, as it will not allow

organizations to capitalize on all that they have experienced

and learned over the past few months. Instead, we believe

that organizations should embrace *New York Times*

columnist Thomas Friedman's perspective that humans who

want to adapt in an age of acceleration must develop

"dynamic stability." Rather than trying to stop an inevitable

storm of change, Friedman encourages leaders to "build an

eye that moves with the storm, draws energy from it, but

creates a platform of dynamic stability within it."[xliii]

Chapter 5

Digital Marketing, Accelerated IT,

and Artificial Intelligence

Small Businesses Reliance on these technologies is Critical

for Success and Growth.

Without Them, You Will Not Survive!

As data experts around the world analyze markets and provide their thoughts and concerns, related questions keep emerging. What will digital marketing look like when stay at home orders and shutdowns are lifted following the COVID-19 pandemic? What if things don't return to normal? How has the shutdown altered consumers habits and spending preferences? How have lockdown orders changed consumer behavior, and will this create a lasting impact? It's clear that screen time has increased as outdoor activities and group sports became restricted. Does that mean consumers will spend more time shopping online?

Have traditional advertising methods been altered as fewer drivers see billboards, or are exposed to radio ads?

One of the most potent things about digital marketing is that it leverages live video, still photography, audio cues, and can utilize artificial intelligence to create effective ad campaigns. One of the reasons content marketing is so effective is that it focuses on customer experience and retention by interacting with consumers on platforms they are comfortable and familiar with online. This leads to a more organic experience for customers, which can be customized with automated marketing. Another consideration is the ability to pivot your campaigns in real-time while developing digital touch-points.[xliv]

As it becomes more popular, paid digital advertisement is becoming more accessible and cheaper. This is a result of big ad networks generating revenue through their auction systems, and they rely on small businesses to inflate the cost per click (CPC), which in turn forces larger corporations with revenues in the billions to increase their marketing budgets. If these platforms don't have the volume that small businesses provide, they will struggle to maintain profitability from ad revenue. Thus, as all non-essential business shutdown amid the pandemic, it became clear that small businesses would need to improvise and adapt to create new methods for connecting them with potential consumers. The most cost-effective solution has emerged as digital marketing that connects consumers with companies on their phones or tablets.

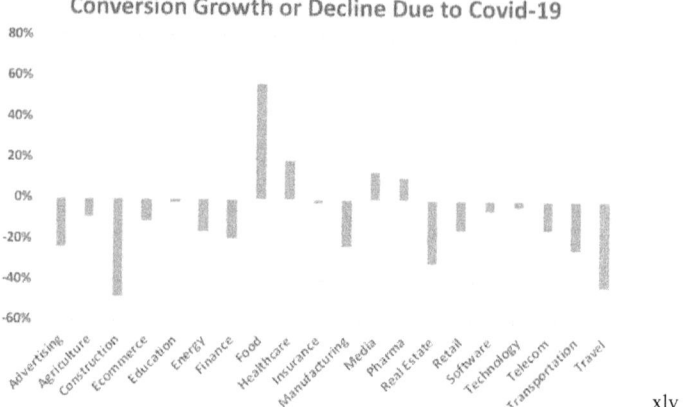

Conversion Growth or Decline Due to Covid-19

xlv

This graph reflects the jobless rates across some of the largest industries and illustrates that some markets are in free-fall. By utilizing cutting edge marketing tools with accessible costs, we can attempt to revitalize specific sectors. The reality is everything has changed, and the only way many small businesses will be able to survive is if they pivot their advertising methods or establish marketing practices if it's previously been an undeveloped portion of their business.

So, let's explore one of the most effective marketing methods, which is deceptively simple and remarkably potent. Give consumers something for **FREE**. Analyze your product or service and identify something you can afford to give away for free like a sticker if you have a physical product, consultation, or evaluation of services you provide. People appreciate that you're sacrificing something for their benefit and develop an inclination to continue purchasing from or working with a vendor they've built an empathetic connection. This empathy and need for connection are especially crucial during these unprecedented times as humans have increasingly been stuck inside and craving interaction. An unintended benefit of this is also that it will increase your overall traffic and generate more clicks and ultimately more conversions. Ad prices are trending down, which means businesses can harness the power of digital marketing without going broke trying to generate revenue. Online consumption of content has seen a considerable increase during shutdown measures with some popular streaming services even having to throttle streaming speeds to meet demands. So clearly, traffic is up, and advertisers are taking note. If you average global sales and demands during the pandemic, you will see a 71% increase in ROI for digital marketing.[xlvi]

Paid ads are becoming the best way for small businesses to promote themselves, create brand awareness, and increase revenue and conversions. With current market conditions, there's more ad space available, and access is more accessible than ever before.

After the first week of pandemic shutdowns, many industries found themselves in trouble, and while that remains mostly true, some have seen bounce backs or corrections. The airline and tourism industries have been some of the hardest hit. But, for online businesses, there has been an uptick, especially if your business partners with a company like Affirm to offer instalment payment plans and encourage consumer spending. This also applies to consultants who can offer a suite of services with a structured payment plan allowing their clients to ease some of the financial burdens they would find with upfront or on-arrival payment. These incentives create a mutually beneficial relationship and encourage consumers to purchase as they face a lower fee in the short term. This can be one of the most effective ways to boost conversion rates in a time where many consumers are looking to online shopping as not only a necessity but a form of entertainment.[xlvii]

Entrepreneurs have always faced challenges, and launching an online business in 2020 delivers a unique set of challenges. There is more competition than ever in the online sector, with new concepts being brought to market every day. These markets are often already saturated, and it can be challenging to set yourself apart from the pack. Due to both of these factors, consumers have nearly unlimited options when it comes to choosing a purveyor. So, before you start to build your website or design the UX for your online store, you need to land on a product or service you can be passionate about. This decision will impact every subsequent decision and influence your design, branding, and corporate voice. You'll need to start developing a brand name, find a website builder, or learn website design yourself. Define a marketing plan, and if you are going to implement loyalty programs or other customer incentives. Implement fulfilment and shipping systems before you go to market. While each of these is an individual part of the process, they are all equally important and mean nothing if you don't have a great product at the end of the day.

Choosing a Product

No matter what industry you're in, there are two product types, niche and commoditized. Niche products appeal to a specific customer base and require a deeper understanding of your target demographic and product. Niche products can be customized, handmade, or rare, which makes them some of the most sought-after products online. Commoditized products make up the bulk of what's for sale online, think items found on large websites like Amazon or Walmart. These products are food items, household goods, clothes, sports equipment or things that are used widely for day to day purposes.

Some entrepreneurs choose to offer a combination of niche and commoditized products to increase their base and generate more revenue. If one chooses only to offer commoditized products it can be challenging to create a unique brand that offers something that more prominent retailers can get to market at a lower cost. Large retailers can purchase vast quantities of items thus lowering their bottom line which makes it difficult for a small business to compete with their pricing on everyday household items like paper towels, so it's best to explore who you plan to market to and what their unique desires are when choosing a product for your online business. By establishing your brand identity with a combination of niche and commoditized items, you will be able to develop your online presence while building a customer base.

We can use Whole Earth Provision as an excellent example of a company that targets a niche audience while still providing products for broader audiences like Chaco footwear, YETI Coolers, The North Face and Patagonia.[xlviii] Their retailers also sell niche products targeting rock climbers and selling climbing shoes, chalk bags, and more targeted products. This combination of broad appeal and niche products allows them to draw in audiences from both a technical standpoint and people looking for brands associated with these activities. This mix is also beneficial for companies' online outlets.

Let's breakdown the process of choosing the right product for your company by identifying or creating products that remove a pain-point or solve a problem.

Look at your daily routine, what is something that could help you throughout the day or make tasks easier or more enjoyable? Perhaps it's working out with headphones, but the cable makes it difficult. Wireless headphones have become a popular option for exercise and commuting. If you can identify and solve a problem, you will be able to create a successful brand or product; it's that simple.

Solutions don't need to be complicated or challenging; they require ease of use and convenience, and often the easier they are, the more successful they become.

Opportunities for products exist in numerous forms. You can improve and existing products with new features or applications. You may see an untapped market for products that have applications in other industries. Perhaps a product needs to be re-positioned in a different market with unique marketing or brand voice.

By thinking like a consumer, you will be able to provide your customers with a product and authentic buying experience that brings value to their life. Entrepreneurship is by no means easy, it takes hard work, dedication, and creativity to establish and build a brand, but it can be one of the most rewarding projects in one's life. The struggle and sacrifice of running your own business will help you build a compelling brand message that connects with your customers in an authentic and meaningful way. Your emotional investment in your product will drive many decisions and ultimately create your core values and mission. Besides, your story is often what sets you apart from your competitors.

You've identified a product with the potential to create solutions for consumer's problems that is in line with your passion. Now you need to create a compelling brand message that will make you stand out in the ultra-competitive commerce market. To develop a popular and impactful brand, you'll have to research and fundamentally understand your demographic. Your message needs to connect with customers inspiring their first purchase and retains them as repeat buyers. The goal is to build a loyal customer base focused on your audience's identity.

Develop a Marketing Brief

- How does your target demographic communicate organically?
- Where is your product positioned in the market?

131

- What is your web presence going to convey? Find a thematic, consistent color scheme, easily navigable layout, and create calls to action throughout your website.[xlix]

One of the most crucial things in developing a brand is emphasizing how you fit into the community, and this is critical to building your online identity. If your customer base can't relate to your brand or product, you've got no foundation to build upon.

Identify and get in on trends early. By taking advantage of emerging markets, you can establish your brand as one of the innovators and pioneers in the industry and gain a majority of the market share. This gives small businesses a huge advantage as you can utilize SEO from the beginning.

Think of products that have been trending in recent years and identify where they started and if you are passionate about similar things.

Another consideration is developing a brand or product around guilty pleasures or vices. Consumers build deep loyalties to brands that cater to their vices. Tobacco, Alcohol, and fast-food companies all deliver products that are not good for people per se, but their consumers' devotion is deep and often unwavering. People don't buy different brands of cigarettes and even identify themselves by their particular choice. This comes back to serving niche markets as well. Say you love ice cream, explore a way to innovate within that market, and you'll find a brand your passionate about.

Another popular way to build a community through your brand is to donate a portion of your profits to a charitable organization that is in line with your market's audience and goals. For example, if you're a dog food brand, emphasize that 1% of profits goes back to the ASPCA, this creates a connection with your audience and will build loyalty and dedication.

10 Niche Products Trending in 2020

1. Convenient, on-the-go, health food
2. Craft Beer/ Cocktail delivery or pickup (Non-Alcoholic too)
3. Monthly subscription boxes that focus on specific activities (Fishing, Clothing, Makeup, Skincare, etc.)
4. CBD Products from oils to edibles
5. Innovative wedding bands for men
6. Personal notebooks and custom planners
7. Dog and cat food
8. Cruelty-Free skin and beauty products

9. Photography equipment, especially drones

10. Shaping undergarments

Be Prepared to Identify Business Opportunities All Over the Place

Creativity is essential for entrepreneurs, and successful business owners find inspiration from everything. It's vital to analyze the world around you, pay close attention to how people around you behave. What shifts can you identify? How can you make others' lives better? Who is buying certain products? What are the emerging industries?

By keeping up with contemporary culture, you will be able to identify new business opportunities continually. Evaluate your thoughts and identify your passions and strengths. Some people find themselves with a natural disposition towards marketing but cringe at the thought of launching a fundraising campaign. In contrast, others have no idea how to connect with potential consumers but thrive in cold calls.

Find your strengths and pinpoint them. Start to compile all of your resources and prepare to bring your online business to life. Streamlined goals and an organized plan will set your business up for long term success.

How to Start Your Online Store

You've identified a product, but the work has just begun. Before you build your website, you still have some more steps before you're ready to go live.

- Conduct thorough market research and identify trends
- Ensure that your products are ready to sell
- Focus on a target demographic and get to know their preferences intimately
- Research which platforms you will utilize for your eCommerce (your site, Amazon, eBay, or other platforms)

- Create compelling, actionable content to sell your product

- Implement a sales and marketing strategy to target your potential customers

Launching an eCommerce store is by no means an easy endeavor, but with a clear plan and strategy, you can build a successful business online.

Resources for Information about Starting Your Online Business

I've compiled some compelling articles regarding establishing your online brand, and each article will allow you to develop your model and scope for your online business.

One of the most important decisions you make is which platform you are going to utilize for your store so read the following articles to make your you have made the best decision when you land on your preferred commerce site.

- BigCommerce vs Shopify: The Clash of The E-Commerce Titans. Who Will Win? (Digital.com)[l]

- Best Ecommerce Websites For Design Inspiration: 22 Award-Winning Examples (2019)[li]

- Need Ecommerce Business Ideas? 27 Experts Give You Their Best Online Store Opportunities For 2019[lii]

- 26 Top Trending Products to Sell Online At Your eCommerce & Dropshipping Store in 2019 (Cloudways)[liii]

- Top Ecommerce Niches of 2019 (Ecomdash)[liv]

Ecommerce is not that different from traditional business, and some essential business basics are critical to your success, these articles take a deeper dive into business basics.

- How to Master Product Photography on a Tight Budget (We Did it With Less Than $50)[lv]

- How to Write a Returns and Exchanges Policy That Grows Sales[lvi]

- The Complete Guide to Writing Product Copy That Sells Itself[lvii]

- 27 Experts Give You Ideas For Ecommerce Businesses[lviii]

Creating a visually appealing and easily navigable website is crucial to your success online. Customers are drawn to sites that not only appear professional but are easy to buy from; these articles explore how to design a website that functions at a high level while also dazzling consumers with their aesthetic.

- 22 Ecommerce Sites For Awesome Website Design Inspiration[lix]

- Get Inspiration From Innovative Ecommerce Brands[lx]

- Ecommerce Store Inspiration: Designs We Love + Sites With Awesome Functionality[lxi]

- Your Guide To Ecommerce Themes: How To Choose The Right Design For Your Online Store[lxii]

Once you've got your design and site ready to go, it's imperative to get website content is written, product photography, and direct calls to action, these articles will allow you to learn how to make your online store stand out in a sea of competitors.

- How to Master Product Photography on a Tight Budget (We Did it With Less Than $50)[lxiii]

- The Complete Guide to Writing Product Copy That Sells Itself[lxiv]

- How to Create eCommerce Product Videos That Drive Traffic[lxv]

- 17 Best Ecommerce Product Video Examples[lxvi]

The next step in the process is choosing how you will

accept payments, and your method is crucial

to increase conversions by making checkout quick and

easy, check out these links for more.

- How To Accept Credit Card Payments Online in 2019: What Are Your Best Options?[lxvii]

- Payment Gateways: Keeping Your Ecommerce Transactions Safe + Customers Happy (2019)[lxviii]

- These Brands Make It Big By Using Amazon Pay (Benefits + Examples)[lxix]

- Seven eCommerce Merchants Discuss Apple Pay's Growing Benefits (2019)[lxx]

- 6 Surprising Ways Accepting Mobile Payments Helps Businesses (Square)[lxxi]

- 8 Things to Know About Payment Security (PNC)[lxxii]

In this day and age, cybersecurity is one of the most critical factors for keeping your customer's data secure and having a trustworthy website, the following articles explore how to protect your customers.

- Everything You Need to Know About PCI Compliance and How to Achieve It[lxxiii]

- What is the ISO Certification? ISO Meaning and BigCommerce's ISO 27001 Achievement[lxxiv]

So now that you've got your site live and products are shipping out let's explore how to handle post-conversion issues like returns and exchanges.

- How to Write a Returns and Exchanges Policy That Grows Sales[lxxv]

- Next Steps After The Sale: Your Guide to Small Business Shipping[lxxvi]

- Calculating Ecommerce Shipping Costs: Rates & Fees[lxxvii]

- Shipping Sales Tax in 2019: Taxability Examples, Laws & More[lxxviii]

- eCommerce Fulfillment: 3 Strategies To Fulfill Online Orders (2019)[lxxix]

- Ecommerce Shipping: Strategies, Solutions & Best Practices (Advanced)[lxxx]

- Ecommerce Warehousing 101: Best Practices + Checklist (2019)[lxxxi]

- Dropshipping in 2019: Does It Actually Work? (Pros + Cons)[lxxxii]

- Startup Fulfillment Services by ShipBob[lxxxiii]

Once you've made your first sale and your site is fully polished, the next step is to start generating traffic and building brand visibility.

- 30 Ways to Drive Traffic to Your Ecommerce Store[lxxxiv]

- How to Create eCommerce Product Videos That Drive Traffic[lxxxv]

- Ecommerce SEO Guide: How Online Stores Can Drive Organic Traffic in 2019[lxxxvi]

Conversion is the key to a successful commerce site so let's explore how you can create the ideal customer experience on your website.

- How to Use Psychology and Sales Triggers to Double Your Conversion Rate[lxxxvii]

- The Science of Emotional Buying and What Marketers Can Do About It[lxxxviii]

- How to Remove Friction From Your Buyer Journey[lxxxix]

- 3 Ways to Use Customer Data Right Now to Increase Conversions[xc]

- 31 Email Marketing Tips to 5x Conversion[xci]

- 6 Ideas for Landing Pages[xcii]

Customer retention is one of the most important keys to a successful online business, and these articles identify keys to marketing and retaining customers.[xciii]

- How to Set Up an Ecommerce Loyalty Program[xciv]

- The 3 Phases of Ecommerce Personalization[xcv]

Track your Growth, have accurate forecasts and build a model for how your business will grow.

- Why Conversion Rate is the One Metric That Determines Your Success[xcvi]

Diversification is one of the best ways to find success in eCommerce, and most brands develop multiple revenue streams. The hard truth is modern consumers have access to many retailers online, and building loyalty is difficult when convenience, access, and price are the key components. Selling on traditional commerce sites like Amazon, eBay, and Google is essential. Still, it's also necessary to consider utilizing social media like Facebook, Pinterest, Twitter, and Instagram to draw customers to your site and increase conversions. These articles explore how to use both traditional online retailers as well as social media sites to build organic engagement.

- The Definitive Guide to Selling on Amazon[xcvii]

- Sell on Amazon from BigCommerce's Central Control Panel[xcviii]

- Create a Profitable Google Shopping Campaign[xcix]

- The Complete Guide to Advertising on Facebook[c]

- Sell Seamlessly on Facebook with One-Click[ci]

- How to Grow an Engaged, Ready-to-Buy Community on Pinterest[cii]

- Sell on Pinterest Across Devices[ciii]

- The Complete Ecommerce Guide to Twitter Advertising[civ]

- How Your Business Can Make Money Selling on Instagram[cv]

- Shopping on Instagram Results Are In: Brands Report +1,416% Traffic, +20% Revenue[cvi]

- Instagram Influencer Marketing: The Organic Superfood You Need To Fuel Your Ecommerce Store[cvii]

COVID-19 Impacts, Effects, and Opportunities

As stay at home orders and social distancing impact retail online shopping and eCommerce is becoming increasingly popular, now may be an excellent time to explore establishing an online store. The pandemic has changed how retailers engage with consumers and how marketing required a new tone and connection to consumers. Confident marketing strategies during this time require nuance and a deeper understanding of your customer base.

The coronavirus pandemic is continually evolving and requires online retailers to stay up to date with safety concerns and develop an earnest connection with consumers while meeting their needs and desires. I'm going to explore some ways to utilize different forms of marketing to build your online business during these uncertain times.

Paid Strategies to Build Organic Engagement on Social Media Platforms

If you can afford to spend some of your marketing budget on paid social media strategies, it can be one of the best ways to build visibility, drive traffic, and increase conversions. With the shutdown, consumers are spending a lot more time on their phones and social media platforms; due to this fact getting in front of these consumers is critical. I have owned and operated a professional advertising, branding and social media marketing company for over twenty years. There are thousands of digital agencies to choose from. The most important thing is to select an agency that is experienced and ethical. Many times agencies do not perform and it is difficult for the

CEO or owner to evaluate when a digital agency is effective. Now it is very simple question, are they generating leads and conversions? It does take 3-6 months to really let any good marketing strategy work. By the sixth month if there is no response I think you need to re-evaluate if this is the agency with the competence level you need or contact me at Deborah@djs3llc.com and I will help you evaluate your position. Developing a scope for your marketing plan that will align audiences and build your brand across social media platforms is the goal.[cviii]

Pay Per Click Marketing Strategies

If you choose a product that needs to simply get in front of consumers like an everyday household item, pay per click (PPC) marketing may be one of the best marketing strategies for your business. With an approach based on sales history, competitor analysis, research, and cross channel insights, you can develop a productive PPC ecosystem that will build robust conversion. Utilize

keyword optimization to integrate data-driven tech to build

your brand and see how consumers are spending during the

pandemic.

Utilize Everyday Necessities to Increase Sales

As shutdowns are impacting traditional brick and mortar

retail amid the COVID-19 pandemic, one strategy is to

utilize sites like Amazon and Walmart in your sales

strategy by developing funnel click strategies. Amazon's

marketing techniques have evolved into a sophisticated

ecosystem that can be used to drive sales, and everyday

items have become some of the best sellers on the site.

Competition on the larger platforms is robust, so it's

essential to set your business apart by finding your niche,

whether that's price, visibility, or access and develop a

robust marketing strategy based on your unique selling

proposition.

The King of eCommerce-Search Engine Optimization (SEO)

You've likely already heard that you need to optimize your search results, but what exactly does that mean? At its basic level, SEO is having keywords appear on your site so that when consumers search for a product or service, they are driven to your website. One of the best ways to increase SEO results is to start a blog with topics that are relevant to your product so that keywords appear organically, and frequently across your platforms. It can take months or even years to start generating engagements due to SEO, so it's essential to take it seriously and add content frequently so that users are driven to your site. Blogs have another strength in building your brand, and that is creating a connection for you and your consumers while also giving you a way to give your brand a voice. Having an engaging presence on social platforms also aids SEO by allowing you to utilize trending hashtags and topics to gain visibility.

A frequently asked questions page also helps with SEO by providing a space to implant keywords frequently in a way that feels organic. Explore ways to build content on your website for SEO and organic engagement to drive visibility and increase conversions.

Utilize Multiple Channels and Platforms to Build a Successful eCommerce Business

This guide has given you the resources and knowledge you need to identify a product, develop a brand, and build an eCommerce site. By following these steps, any aspiring entrepreneur can develop their own brand and successful business. The importance of utilizing multiple platforms from traditional online retailers like Amazon to emphasizing social media presence cannot be underestimated, but that's not to say it's impossible. The key to success as an online retailer is persistence, consistency, and a comprehensive plan. One of the most critical aspects of establishing your eCommerce website is the ability to evolve and adapt as markets change and consumer demands develop.

Successful online brands don't stick to one platform or channel and build their brand and voice across all available outlets. By connecting with your customers and building organic engagement, you can create a loyal base and build customer retention, which is key to any successful business. Blogs and social media platforms allow you to develop a unique voice that sets you apart from your competitors while establishing a relationship with your target demographic.

As with any business, the importance of marketing cannot be downplayed, and developing an effective marketing strategy early on will allow you to analyze your past success and forecast future campaigns and expansion. Get to truly know your customer base and utilize trends and shifts in opinion to maintain engagement, which will increase traffic and repeat customers. Build a robust website to improve SEO, which is critical to differentiate yourself from your competitors. Identify your space and build an online presence to find success as an online retailer, and the possibilities are limitless.[cix]

Chapter 6

Bankruptcy is not an Option for Small Business

There are Fangs in These Laws and it Is Expensive,

Go Figure!

It is logical that if your basic needs have not been met like health and fear of death or trauma, businesses cannot function. In the case of a global pandemic, it stands to reason we will see a tsunami of bankruptcies big and small. The beginning tidal wave of bankruptcy is happening as we speak. In Book I, I call bankruptcy a scourge and not for small business. According to data retrieved from the US Court System (USCourt.gov), bankruptcy reported a decrease from year to year in June 2019. Bankruptcy filing fell 0.3 percent for the 12 months starting June 2018 to June 2019 totaling 773,361 compared with 775,578. Business filings increased by 1.1 percent.[cx] So, there was some trouble brewing, especially in the retail sector in the same time frame.[cxi]

The following bankruptcy filings statistics are available online.[cxii]

aacer

Month					Chapter 11 Filings Nationwide					
	2020	2019	2018	2017	2016	2015	2014	2013	2012	2011
January	631	366	367	402	494	523	392	488	750	788
February	649	685	425	407	485	364	485	623	757	770
March	530	449	774	471	450	414	567	598	687	789
April	562	444	394	576	681	409	690	710	666	802
May	723	487	448	581	613	502	431	542	717	722
June	609	424	310	601	503	366	483	499	545	761
July	643	423	415	333	359	645	359	540	704	596
August	-	450	364	499	368	534	360	604	653	711
September	-	420	312	446	366	337	377	584	525	697
October	-	530	557	317	406	431	390	528	550	687
November	-	449	662	435	387	392	298	488	670	604
December	-	392	456	703	338	401	357	397	565	748
Total	4.247	5.519	5.484	5.771	5.450	5.318	5.189	6.601	7.789	8.675

"Cases included in totals represent only commercial business bankruptcy filings" [cxiii]

In the table above it reported a total of 5,519 business bankruptcies or chapter 11s for all of 2019. So far in the first six months of 2020 there have been 4,247 businesses already filing for bankruptcy protection. Right before publication of this book the numbers through to July took a

48% increase in business bankruptcy. I discussed this at length and will clarify any new laws in this chapter about Chapter 11 business bankruptcy. I feel adamant that bankruptcy is not for mom and pop businesses, and it is not for any business, not generating revenue. So many times, I hear the hardship from people who just did not know and filed under their attorneys' recommendation and ended up in a draconian federal filing. The ramifications are so complicated and vast, it could place you in personal bankruptcy, and if those schedules are not filled out with complete accuracy, you can place yourself in serious legal jeopardy. There is a prediction that bankruptcies will be so vast a problem that the courts may not be able to handle the caseload.

One of the best ways to create a robust business environment to incentivize people to start and stay in business is to have lenient bankruptcy laws. We need to send the message that it's okay to fail, especially in the wake of COVID-19 and the sudden and abrupt slowing of the economy and the lack of demand for many non-essential products and services.

"Entrepreneurs power the American economy. They enter and exit in a continuous, harmonious process that Joseph Schumpeter in 1942 called creative destruction, the essential fact about capitalism." I do not think even Schumpeter factored into his theory the catastrophic effects of such a physical threat like the spread of a deadly pandemic.[cxiv]

When he wrote this, one-third of new businesses died in the first two years; when I started my business in 1989, about 50 percent were able to survive to year five or beyond. Now, most fail, and it is estimated as high as 90 percent in some states. The federal bankruptcy laws in Schumpeter's day were written so that the entrepreneur could bounce back. This policy is no longer available. With the disparity of income, a shrinking consumer base, and lack of capital and investment, our policymakers refuse to see that the deck is stacked against entrepreneurs. Our Congressional Leaders complacence with monopolies and no-resolve to instituting effective anti-trust laws leaves small business entrepreneurs at a grave disadvantage. As a result, the numbers of bankruptcies have more than doubled since the 2008 worst level.

Now the majority fails to survive. Until 2008, new business births always exceeded deaths. Now the number of deaths to small enterprises is at a frightening level. With data unavailable for 2020 this percentage will increase drastically.

Despite such odds, the number of new entrants has been increasing slowly in the first and second quarters of 2020, probably because the US did not seem to take heed to the coming pandemic. How do we help this increase during and after COVID-19? How do we encourage the serial entrepreneur to try, resurfacing, again and again, if he or she so desires? And, the millions in survival mode during and after the pandemic need to regain strength in a continuously fragile and changing economy. How do we coax them to try again? Remember, small businesses account for more than 99 percent of all enterprises in the United States, close to 47.3 percent of all employment, and 65 percent of new hires. Small business success is tied to our economic recovery and the health of our nation.

Much of the national policy debate about small business focus, rightly, on firms that can survive. Taxes, healthcare costs, capital growth, and the like are generated by businesses that have more than 20-50, employees on their payrolls, and investment options. But what about firms that don't make it? How do we treat entrepreneurs who fail? What is the lasting effect on our American psychic and Brand America? The latest research suggests that this may be a turning point in the US as so many companies are filing for bankruptcy or merely closing their doors at an alarming rate.

A Shift in Priorities

Over the years, America's personal bankruptcy system has served as a hedge against entrepreneurial failure. When businesses fail, entrepreneurs can shield some of their assets from creditors by filing under Chapter 7 of the federal bankruptcy laws, the usual route for consumer filings. In fact, nearly 20 percent of all personal filings list business debts, and the value of business debts represents half the total liabilities of bankruptcy filers. But, entrepreneurs are seldom the focus of debates about bankruptcy reform, because the process rarely distinguishes consumers from small business owners. This lack of understanding is the flaw in these new policies.[cxv]

America's bankruptcy law is rooted in the "fresh start"—the idea that honest debtors experiencing a spot of bad luck, such as temporary job loss, illness, or divorce, are capable of putting the past behind them and moving on. This concept works exceptionally well for owners of small businesses. By wiping out debts and pardoning failure, American bankruptcy gives the entrepreneur a chance to bounce back and even be worry-free, if he really screws up, and an opportunity to learn from his or her mistakes.

It's no surprise that these laws—seen as lenient not just by creditors but by our policymakers influenced by these creditors' lobbyist—have increasingly become a subject of debate in recent times.

There is a growing fear that the system is too harsh to

debtors, and there is evidence that this could be, potentially,

crushing our entrepreneurship. The number of Americans

seeking relief from creditors each year has more than

doubled in the past decade to almost two million. This

steady and rapid rise in bankruptcy filings has coincided

with a generally robust economy as is reflected in data from

the Small Business Administration.

These figures are a clear alert that the disparity in income

on Main Street to the robust growth of tech and Wall street

is affecting small business owners and their consumer base

way before the Great Recession and now the global

pandemic. Yet, either our lawmakers never saw these

parallels, or large corporations and banks blinded them.

Unfortunately, I believe we know the answer.

Under pressure from creditor groups, including banks and

credit card companies, Congress, in 2005, passed the

Bankruptcy Abuse, Fraud, Prevention, and Consumer Protection Act, which make debtors jump through many more bureaucratic hoops to get relief. Signing the act, President Bush said, "In recent years, too many people have abused the bankruptcy laws. They've walked away from debts, even when they had the ability to repay them. This has made credit less affordable and less accessible." Yet, in an attempt to re-gauge the imbalance, the debate on bankruptcy has neglected implications that legislation misjudged entrepreneurial behavior.

Does bankruptcy regulation affect entrepreneurship? My own research, along with that of Michelle J. White, professor of economics at the University of California at San Diego, answers with an unequivocal yes. Studying variations in-laws across the country, we find that states that, more extensively, protect the assets of those filing for bankruptcy, have a higher percentage of business start-ups and survival rates. Thus, the more a state forgives its debtors, the greater the entrepreneurial dynamism in that state.

Entrepreneurship is often a process of trial and error. No one would accuse Henry Ford of being an unsuccessful entrepreneur. But Ford started two car companies that failed before he struck gold with the Ford Motor Company. Sometimes we fail at no fault of our own, as is the case for over 5.8 million citizens and businesses that filed between 2008 and 2012 (reference chart, below), just after the so-called Great Recession. If you know that your home and personal property will be protected no matter what the outcome of your venture, you are more likely to take the risk of starting a business in the first place and to try again if you don't succeed. States like Texas, Nevada, and Delaware, with high personal bankruptcy exemptions, offer a better environment for businesses than Maryland or

Virginia, with relatively low exemptions. The right to go bust is an insurance policy against financial disaster. These policies have undergone drastic changes since 2005. States are less likely to see high entrepreneurship rates if their exemptions are lower than those of neighboring states. After all, entrepreneurs are free to move across state lines and take advantage of more lenient exemptions. Just as people vote with their feet by moving to states with lower taxes and better schools, entrepreneurs move to states with better bankruptcy regulations and better business conditions.

These findings warn that bankruptcy reform must proceed with care and especially with a better understanding of the role bankruptcy plays for small businesses. But, the 2005 law seems to be moving in the wrong direction. It introduced a slew of new provisions to make it harder for individuals to file for bankruptcy or businesses to survive once they have filed. According to the latest data, only 10 percent of all companies that file Chapter 11 actually survive. Most are forced later to dissolve under a Chapter 7 filing—death at the end of a prolonged illness.

For instance, only those with incomes below the state median can claim asset protection under Chapter 7; others must either devise a repayment plan out of future earnings under Chapter 11 or not file at all. Exemptions have been lowered for certain assets, and debtors need to undergo credit counselling prior to filing, a process that can be costly, humiliating, and, for many business owners, useless. A better approach would be to let creditors work through the market to ensure that debtors with a bad credit history or risky entrepreneurial ventures are given loans at higher interest rates. Also, creditors could issue more secured debt to ensure repayment.

If entrepreneurs of failed businesses are denied debt discharge, they may take up safer wage and salary jobs rather than risk starting up a new venture. We can all end up working for big global conglomerates or the government. Another unintended consequence of the legislation, therefore, maybe the loss of another Henry Ford, Steve Jobs, or Bill Gates, me, or you, or anyone with a dream and a vision, however big or small. And lowering the level of asset protection provided to homes and personal property means even higher stakes for start-ups, deterring would-be entrepreneurs from risking creative destruction. In the case of the impact of the 2005 laws, it could mean a change from creative destruction to the extinction of the American entrepreneur. With fewer entrepreneurs, we move toward socialism and jeopardize the great experiment upon which democracy was built.

For the millions of firms on survival mode, the need to
retool and resuscitate your business is of paramount
importance before you slip into bankruptcy because of this
draconian policy. This is why I call bankruptcy reform one
of the social imperatives of our times. The pandemic and
the anticipated tsunami of bankruptcies to follow may force
Congress to finally take a look at how important it will be
to the country getting back to stability. There is a
profoundly negative impact from these drastic changes in
the law on small-firms' entry decisions and current firms'
options to regroup. It is simply scary as hell out there, and
bankruptcy has caused untold suffering to millions of
entrepreneurs.

A sad irony of the 2005 legislation is that, while many
countries are learning from an American system that is seen
widely as the world's most friendly to entrepreneurs,
America seems not to be heeding its own lessons. One of

the reasons I wrote this book is because I saw from the data on bankruptcy that the American dream is dying because of these very policies. The total lack of understanding or concern of our lawmakers is why we need to develop a system or network to help each other navigate through these tumultuous times. We also need to communicate openly the consequences of policies that kill the dreams of so many.

Do we really want to move toward a system where failure is feared, and the entrepreneurial spirit takes a beating at every turn? Or, on the other hand, do we want to tell our entrepreneurs that there is hope on its way when they are in SOS and provide the tools and support needed to get out of this mess through the help of an open-source of resources.

Enter the Lobbyists

History teaches us that entrepreneurship involves a process of learning and experimentation; failure may well be a crucial part of this process. These quantum structural changes are complex and involve great risk even more so than in the past for small enterprise. In order to survive the sharp decline in demand because of COVID-19 businesses need new markets, testing new ways of developing products, communicating in new media, reinventing yourself and trying something completely new—these are all about innovation and experimentation. As a society and an economy, our best asset may be our ability to accept and forgive. So, each time we tighten our bankruptcy laws in response to the legions of lawyers, large banks, and credit card companies, we have to wonder if we are not, inadvertently, reducing America to Rome.

Mark Leibovich's book, *This Town*, takes down what he calls the creatures who infest our nation's capital. Christopher Buckley's review states, "*This Town* reads like the endgame chapters of Gibbon's *Decline and Fall of the Roman Empire*." In it, he discusses the tectonic changes that have occurred in the past 50 years, number one being the near-complete takeover of our elected officials by lobbyists of special interests. President Trump promised to clean the swamp. Unfortunately, the only key legislation he passed was the 2018 tax cuts that mostly helped the top 3 percent of incomes. "Now 50 percent of Senators and 42 percent of Congressmen join the ranks of influence peddlers because the cash rewards are so large and it is their bounty for their largess while they were in public service."

How can we expect our elected officials to govern and enact policy that will perpetuate our entrepreneurship when it is clear for whom they are really working?

Leibovich goes on to write that corporate America, mostly Wall Street and the large banks, have tripled the amount of money they spend on lobbying and public affairs. Along with that is the tsunami of dollars thrown at presidential campaigns by so-called PACs and mega-donors of over 2 billion dollars. Whom are we kidding? This is corruption at the highest level. We are literally rotting from the inside out. Yet, these are the very lawmakers that have no mercy when a small business—with limited resources and facing an insurmountable shift in our economic system find themselves in debt and struggling. I guess we should have known. But, so many of us did not see it coming and are ill prepared for the amount of capital needed for the length of a pandemic or natural disaster.

The Bankruptcy Process

This chapter is a wakeup call that bankruptcy is not an option for small business, but a scourge. All of the talk of a "fresh start" and a "salvation" is the language of law firms who want your business in order to collect large fees. Once you sign their engagement letter, the veil begins to be lifted to expose a brutal process. Many people commit suicide, need counselling, or never start a business again as a result. Bankruptcy law, seemingly by design, is one of the most confusing areas of the law. It is billed as a protection, but in fact, it is a destructive process both financially and psychologically. It can thrust a small business because of inadequate counsel into greater expense and could last for years, which is why I became so alarmed at the sheer numbers of our entrepreneurial brothers and sister going through this hell every year. I believe it is because there is a complete lack of awareness of how vial this process can be for most businesses that file under Chapter 7 or 11

Protection. Even the name is misleading.

Under Chapter 7 of the bankruptcy code, you liquidate your

business, and the sale of those assets helps pay your

creditors. The area that gets grey is that most large

institutions—especially credit card companies in their fine

print—hold you personally liable for any business expenses

even though the card is under your business name. Hence,

you are then forced to shift course and file on a personal

level, and that places every personal asset in jeopardy of

liquidation, including the shirt off your back.

Unfortunately, asset protection should begin the day you

start your business or decide on the status of your company.

If your counsel does not explain this thoroughly and you

are not forthcoming, or if you don't include even the paper

clips on the filing schedule, then the new law states you are committing federal fraud and could serve up to 20 years in prison. I'll bet most lawyers selling you ongoing bankrupt don't tell you that or veil the process until you sign the engagement letter or perhaps even more egregiously fail to mention it after you file."

They go as far as assigning a Trustee of the courts who gets a "commission" for finding you in a compromising situation. They could spend years suing you for questionable assets, and many businesses relinquish assets simply because there are no resources to defend the assets in question. This is what most business owners are not aware of. During the time a business owner feels compelled to file; generally, he or she is too humiliated and demoralized to ask around as to who is the best attorney his fellow associates may know in order to submit such a complex and serious filing. We all know that without money we cannot find the quality of service we need when we need it. Many struggling entrepreneurs read the veiled sales pitch on the lawyer's website that it is the only way to a "fresh start" and believe it could be the answer to their problems. In fact, it could be the beginning of a process that is short of death by torture.

Chapter 11 bankruptcy states that you can rehabilitate your business by reorganizing your debt in agreement with your creditors. Yet, 95 percent of all companies who file Chapter 11 file for Chapter 7 shortly thereafter because Chapter 11 simply does not provide the help that a struggling small business needs in today's dysfunctional economy. It is such a systemic multi-faceted problem that it only adds to the suffering of small business owners and complicates their already severe problems. For the lawyers who promote it, it simply spells big fees. If they read at all, then they are more than aware of the grim results of such a filing provides for their clients.

Statistics reveal that the few companies that survive Chapter 11 are usually large companies. Donald Trump has declared bankruptcy four times and utilized it as a business tool. He has a legion of attorneys, which, of course, plan for the bankruptcy in advance for many of his development projects in order to increase his own personal wealth. This practice, in general, has driven many small sub-contractors out of business, bidding already on very low margins because of competition and forced later to settle for pennies on the dollar creating the cash-poor scenario that could drive a small contractor over the edge. This is all a legal corporate practice: gaming the system, providing even the bankruptcy code to be written for the benefit of large corporations thanks to lobbyists taking part in the writing of this policy. All are part of business as usual in Washington.

The small businessman cannot resolve all of his problems in Chapter 11 bankruptcy. It is strong medicine for a sick business. For many a small company, it is too strong a medicine that could kill you.

Municipality Bankruptcies

Not only is this systemic problem part of the aftermath of the failure of our financial system resulting in countless home foreclosures, and personal and business bankruptcies, it is also alarmingly on the rise for our municipalities. We have talked about the cause and effect that our failing small businesses have had on so many aspects of our society, but one of the most serious is the bubble I believe that is about to burst and that is, that with the failure of our businesses comes the failure of our municipalities.

In 1980, we had one bankruptcy filing for a municipality. In 2012, for some reason, there is no recording for the fourth quarter, but the three preceding quarters add up to 17. If we average the last five years, the percentage of increase would estimate at least 3 more for fourth-quarter 2012, totaling twenty municipalities filing Chapter 9 bankruptcy.

Twenty US cities are in such financial duress that they are forced to file. In looking at the total US budget and seeing that pensions comprise 22 percent, debt and even municipal loans are bundled and packaged as derivatives; many of our cities do not have the revenue to support this large liability. It can only make one worry about the continued volatility and fragility of who is betting that these loans will burst. We have seen this before in the way the real estate bubble burst, and the last financial bubble burst, setting us on a course that has created the largest disparity in wealth even greater than the Gilded Age. Europe is in far greater straights than the US There is no comfort in feeling we can fend off becoming Greece, however, if we do not make significant and ardent efforts to reclaim and ignite the little engine that could—our small businesses. With the health of our entrepreneurs, we will generate revenue for our cities. It is unconscionable that in 2013, Detroit, once our fourth-largest municipality, has filed Chapter 9 when Congress has been more than happy to spend $3 Billion a month for nation-building in Iraq in the not so distant past. If we cannot save one of our largest cities—one, which housed one of our biggest industries—how are we going to lead the world in capitalism and democracy?

On a more optimistic note, many of our cities are fighting back. In a recent article, Thomas Freidman writes how the most exciting innovation in governance is happening in many American cities. "The country looks so much better from the bottom up." He talks about a metropolitan explosion quoting scholars from the Brookings Institute:

Bruce Katz and Jennifer Bradley expounding on "The Metropolitan Revolution: How Cities and Metros Are Fixing Our Broken Politics and Fragile Economy." There is a trend that many cities are becoming the leaders in the nation by experimenting and taking risks calling it "the inversion of the hierarchy of power."

The Great Recession accelerated the changes to our traditional growth model. "One that exalted consumption overproduction, speculation over investment and waste over sustainability." The new growth model, which most successful cities are practicing, focuses on creating networks.

"They combine skilled labor and knowledgeable workers with universities and technical schools, enhance the quality of infrastructure and high-speed Internet, promote manufacturing, innovation, technology, and advanced service with an eye for exporting all of these." 10 These cities understand that they have to have a sector of their city that is world-class. That is how a twenty-first-century city builds a strong middle class, and prevents the coarsening of society and all of the ills that surround it from taking hold. He is quoted as saying: "Cities and metropolitan areas are on their own! Mired in the partisan division and rancor the federal government seems incapable of taking bold action to restructure our economy and grapple with changing demography and rising inequality." These cities are not waiting for, but are trying to grow, their economies on their own.

This, in fact, is what I have been addressing to small business entrepreneurs before I read Friedman's article. This bottom-up approach and transfer of the hierarchy of power could be the same momentum we can now establish through Business SOS™ and its network of members, sponsors, resources, volunteers and struggling businesses. Business SOS™ is a network established because "Washington and Wall Street seem to be functioning on their own with little or no regard to what is happening to everyday Americans." It is a way for a specific sector of struggling entrepreneurs to get the level of help they need when they need it. Many of us have endured little or no growth for five long years. This can be an economically stressful situation, but bankruptcy, as I have outlined, in many cases, is not the answer.

Business SOS™ is a place entrepreneur can go without hiding from the harsh facts of their reality. There is no judgment or shame, but understanding and assessment of your total corporate DNA in order to protect your business from sliding into bankruptcy. I am a believer that every company is worth saving. As long as the company can eventually profit, there is always a chance to sell and become part of a larger entity that can produce greater challenges and opportunities.

Assets and Protection

One of the preeminent lessons I have learned about business is that right from the beginning, your business and your personal assets need to be protected in case something dreadful happens, and you are forced into bankruptcy. Your business is always vulnerable to litigation and creditors. The boom-bust economies will continue to occur, perhaps even more frequently if Washington doesn't fix the systemic problems that we have discussed. Financial threats are looming all the time and can sink your business as we have seen from our data, effecting millions of businesses. After experiencing five separate economic traumas in the last ten years, we can assume from this pattern they will keep on coming. It is so important that businesses retool and reduce the risk of failure. It has become a necessity to safeguard your enterprise in order to survive in these turbulent times. Hillel Presser, in *Financial Self-Defense*, addresses a trend that is clearly on the rise: to not incorporate or file any business status but to remain a sole proprietor. According to some recent figures from the SBA, this is confirmed from their recent data.

He explains, "There is a case to be made against sole proprietorships as a sole proprietor is personally liable for every business debt." Yet we see an increase in unincorporated self-employment. People are sensing the punishment they will withstand if their corporation fails. When most small businesses now fail, it is putting in jeopardy the entire family's financial security. Presser goes on to say: "It is very foolish, and no business is too small to need to incorporate or form a Limited Liability Company."

Rise of Corporatism

We will develop an app to guide new ventures on this decision-making process. The vision is to garner the help of experienced sponsors, such as Hillel. We will also provide the capability to evaluate the current status of the business filing to keep up with these new economic forces which may be making the simple corporate status for some obsolete and the need to change to an LLC may be a necessity. The complete redesign of your business for twenty-first-century business makes this an important part of the process. And, because so many businesses are failing, we need to impart knowledge and a real understanding of the liabilities you are now facing in continued pervasive survival mode.

This book was written primarily to take the blinders off the eyes of small business owners to encourage them to look at the economic facts and assess their struggles not only within the small microcosm of their current life experience but also through the wide-angle lenses of all the mitigating reasons they cannot change their state of affairs and resuscitate their businesses so easily.

These issues function within two, totally separate economies. The inability of small entrepreneurs to avoid much longer with the devastating effects of bankruptcy may, in fact, change our revered capitalism involuntarily to socialism because of the inequality and the unleveled playing field between large corporations, the enormous wealth of the top one percent of companies and individuals, and the economic distress of the bottom 99 percent. Clearly, what I am saying is that large corporations and monopolies, which are considered the beacon of capitalism, are the strongest and most competitive force. These are the catalyst for more rapid "natural destruction" of smaller competitors. Maybe this is the very reason we are moving toward socialism and not that the bottom half is lazy and

looking to be opportunistic seekers of social services.

Joseph Schumpeter is perhaps best known for his book,

Capitalism, Socialism, and Democracy. His theory is that

capitalism could collapse and be replaced by socialism.[cxvi]

"Creative destruction" is the process in which the old ways

of doing things are endogenously destroyed and replaced

by new ways.[cxvii]

The success of capitalism will lead to a form of corporatism

and foster values hostile to capitalism and democracy in

which there is a lack of equality and a fair playing field for

most innovators or entrepreneurs.[cxviii] He goes on to say:

> The intellectual and social climate needed to allow
>
> entrepreneurship to thrive will not exist in advanced
>
> capitalism or corporatism; it will be replaced by
>
> socialism in some form.[cxix] There will not be a

revolution, but merely a trend in the US to elect policymakers of one stripe or another because of the vast needs of the majority against the power of the minority who cannot compete in a corporatist economy and have less income and need more social services and government jobs and subsidies. He argues that the possible collapse of capitalism from within will come about as democratic governments vote for restrictions upon entrepreneurship that will burden and destroy the capitalist structure; the corporatist will choke off the competitive environment making it hostile to smaller companies. He also emphasizes non-political, evolutionary processes in a society where "liberal capitalism" was evolving into democratic socialism as the result of all of these imbalances. This is a highbrow discussion that simply states the true consequence of inequality for entrepreneurs.

When all the policies are in favor of large corporations and all the regulations are inflicted on all the small organizations the natural trend will be the destruction of democracy and capitalism, as we know it.

This is an economic theory that we can see playing out in our country today. I am obviously on the side of most Americans. Policy does affect our very democracy as we see its vast changes. We have time to correct these trends by taking action. I am offering all of the methods utilized in the development of Business SOS™ in order to correct this unleveled playing field and advantage big corporations now have in the expansion of our capitalism through the harnessing of information technology and globalization. We need to network and harness these capacities, and we can correct this imbalance. These challenges and cycle of businesses are ongoing. Business SOS™ offers the tools to assist small businesses and become part of the new hierarchy of power that is within our reach if we all stop listening to the rhetoric of our politicians and proceed as they did in the early days of this country and help each other like caring and trusted neighbors through the hard times. I am confident we will survive this pandemic but with many fatalities not only in the cost of great entrepreneurs but also in human life which is more of a tragedy.[cxx]

Chapter 7

The Road Map to Your Future

The Strongest Tool to Launch or Revitalize Small

Businesses is a Unique Business Plan

By Kishore Dasaka

Introduction by Deborah J. Scarpa

Kishore and I have been colleagues for over 10 years. Not only have I trusted him with the business plan for Business SOS™ but he and I work closely with many of my clients who proceed with this essential tool to launch a business or revitalize their existing businesses. In the time of COVID-19, the challenges of each small business will be daunting. When under stress it is oftentimes difficult to know in which direction to follow. Do I stay the course or try something related or completely new? Should I simply open up more revenue streams or perhaps go all-digital with virtual product delivery. A business plan lets you see the numbers and projections while providing the most needed research to determine market feasibility. Without one, you are flying blind. With a good business plan, you can create a road map and look at the end result before it happens. Knowledge is power and power for the people is what Business SOS™ is all about. In this chapter, Kishore Dasaka outlines in detail the rationale and the step by step approach of what a comprehensive business plan should encompass. He begins with starting a business and goes on to apply these lessons to existing companies. We have discussed in the previous chapters how important it is to be nimble and stay current. I hope after reading this chapter you are convinced that a well-crafted business plan is critical to start and revitalize your business with clarity, forethought and stability.

Business Plan Expert Kishore Dasaka

Starting a new business is like going on a treasure hunt in the Amazon forests. While there are great rewards to be won in terms of name, fame, and money, there are several dangers and pitfalls, and you could quickly lose your way.

Apart from material and human resources, an essential thing that you need to launch and run your business successfully is money. Whether it is a venture capitalist or a seasoned banker, you need a business plan in order for these investors to see the direction you want to take your company!

What if you already have a business, and you are looking to expand your business, and possibly undertake acquisitions? You will still need lots of capital to fund your expansion, and yes, you will need a business plan for that too.

Why Do You Need a Business Plan?

A business plan is a document that tells the reader about your business, what it does, who its customers are, what its goals are, and how its financials are looking. There are two primary reasons why you need a business plan:

a. **To Raise Capital:** If you are looking to raise capital from friends and family, angel investors, venture capitalists, or bankers, you need a business plan. The business plan should give the reader details on how you would use the financing, how it will meet the company's goals, and how it will increase profits.

From a lender's standpoint, they would want to know how your business will generate cash and repay the loan. Investors would want to see how you will use the money to improve the valuation of the company and help him/her achieve the desired return on the capital invested. Both lenders and investors would usually have access to statistics and research to benchmark your performance, so be sure that your financial projections and assumptions are reasonable.

b. **To Serve as an Operational Guide:** One of the most common reasons for writing a business plan is to use it as an operational guide. The business plan is a blueprint of your business and will provide the necessary direction to navigate the changes in the world of entrepreneurship. It will give a detailed analysis of the company's past, present, and future operations. Hence the business plan must be kept up to date.

Writing a Business Plan for Raising Capital

There are thousands of business plans that are written every day for presenting to investors and lenders. If you are looking to raise capital from lenders or investors, you would need a well-written business plan. You can significantly improve the chances of getting your business funded by considering the following:

- **Fixing your Credit Score:** Whether you are applying for a credit card or a mortgage loan, lenders will want to know your credit score. Analyzing your credit score helps lenders assess the default risk and decide the interest rates. A good credit score will influence the credit that is available to you, the interest rates, and other terms in the loan agreement. It will also demonstrate that you are the right customer. A past default or bankruptcy will often be a 'red-flag' in the credit scoring process and may send out a warning to lenders when they are approving your loan. You will also have to submit your business tax returns (if you own an existing business), and personal tax returns.

- **Collateral:** A collateral is a security that banks utilize in case of a default in repaying the loan. Evaluating your collateral is an essential step in any business loan approval process. The amount and the type of collateral you provide shows your commitment towards repaying the loan on time.

- **Meeting Expectations:** In the case of a bank loan, the expectations are obvious – you have to repay the loan along with interest within the time specified by the lender. You have to ensure that you maintain positive cash flow at all times to allow you to repay the loan and run the business without any operational hiccups. However, if you choose the equity route and raise capital from angel investors or venture capitalists, the consideration is different. Equity investors are often looking at an exit-multiple with a good and viable exit strategy. They will want to know where the business is heading in the short-term and in the long-term. The focus of the equity investors is on profit potential, competitive strength, and long-term sustainability. Unlike lenders, equity investors have a say in how the company operates. This could be in the form of a board-seat or an operating agreement where decisions are taken based on their affirmative approval.

- **Stable Management:** Research shows that one-person companies have had a high rate of failure. In the early 1990s, several tech companies had to shut shop because of poor management, despite having a strong tech team and state-of-the-art development skills. Both lenders and investors would take a close look at the management team, their qualifications, and industry experience.

- **Market-Fit:** You could have a great product, but if there is no demand for the product in the market, there is a bad market-fit. You will have to show your investors and lenders that there is a good demand for your product or service and that the demand will be sustainable. You can prove this by conducting surveys, questionnaires, testimonials, and analyzing your competition. To be considered valid, the responses for the surveys and questionnaires should come from your target market, and not from family and friends. There are secondary market research reports available from sources like IBISWorld, Euromonitor, Mintel, and Statista. You can also use these to prove the existence of the market for your products and services.

- **Uniqueness and Defensibility:** If you are selling products, you should know how and why your product is unique, and how it is different from the ones that are existing in the market. If you are selling a service, you should show how your service will be better than the ones provided by your competitors. This means that you should have secured a proprietary position that is defensible in the market. Defensibility means that your proprietary position is unique and can potentially be protected by copyright, trademark, or a patent.

- **Marketing Plan:** When an investor reviews your business plan, one of the focus areas will be the marketing plan. The marketing plan should clearly define your target customer, how you will reach your customer, and what strategies you will follow to retain and increase your market share. The lender will assess your marketing plan to decide whether you can achieve your revenue targets and generate sufficient cash flows to repay the loan along with interest. An investor will look at your marketing goals, assess the sustainability of your growth in the long-term, and whether or not your company continues to increase its market share to continue driving shareholder values.

- **Financial Projections:** One of the most critical sections in any business plan is your financial projections. Lenders and investors will benchmark your projections against current industry standards and assess the probability of you achieving these projections based on the other parameters discussed earlier. The most common error is overstating revenue and understating expenses. Unreasonable projections will kill the perceived credibility of the entire business plan, and hence you need to present a reasonable financial plan that is achievable.

Begin with the End in Mind

In his book, *7 Habits of Highly Effective People*, Steven R Covey says always begin with the end in mind. Not only does this apply to life in general, but it also applies to a business plan. The "end" in a business plan is a definitive exit strategy. An exit strategy is a plan for success. Developing an exit strategy before you write a business plan will give you the right direction for your business plan and will help make the right decisions for your business.

An exit strategy is like a finish line in a race. Before you begin running, you always need to know where you are expected to finish. Most equity investors (i.e., angel investors, private equity, and venture capitalists) would most likely require a concrete exit strategy as a part of the business plan for any venture that they plan to invest in.

So, what should be your exit strategy? There are no right or wrong exit strategies. There are only different ones. The exit strategy that you use should always fit your goals from the beginning. The right place to start looking for your exit strategy is, to begin with, your long-term goals. Many entrepreneurs often think that the end goal is to retire rich. Some of them would want to sell their business and use the cash to start another venture.

Let's now see some of the common forms of exit strategies:

- **Outright Sale:** An outright sale involves selling the business to an interested and independent buyer. This is very common in technology firms, where bigger firms like Microsoft, Google or Amazon buy the company and technology and integrate the technology with their products and services. In that case, you would want to maximize the net income of the business, so that you get a reasonable exit valuation when the business is taken over by another company.

- **Initial Public Offer:** Initial Public Offer or IPO is a strategy where the firm's stock is listed on a stock exchange like NYSE or NASDAQ. If you are looking to retain control over your company, and yet gain liquidity for your stock, this might be a good option. The complexities and the legal issues involved in this exit are substantial, and it often requires retaining an army of attorneys and accountants to prepare your IPO.

- **Passing on to Family:** This is a good strategy if you are looking to transfer the business to members of your family. In some jurisdictions, this could also be tax efficient. One of the critical success factors of this strategy is that the heirs need to be prepared from early on to take over the business and run the business going forward.

- **Liquidation:** In many businesses, the best option is to simply discontinue the business, sell of its assets, and pay off the creditors. This gives you the most liquidity among all the exit strategies and is one of the commonly preferred exit strategies for people looking to enjoy retired life.

Sources of Finance

In today's world, there are several sources of finance that are available to entrepreneurs. Your choice of financing is essential because that will have a significant impact on the type of exit strategy that you will choose. The kind of funding will also affect the cost of capital, and the associated legal terms and conditions. Let's now see the different sources of finance that are available to an entrepreneur:

- **Owner Financing:** If you manage to invest your savings into the business, this will quality as 'owner financing'. Some of the questions that you will need to ask yourself is, "Do I need additional capital to run my business?"

- **Friends and Family:** In early-stage companies with limited financial history, raising capital from investors or lenders, may not be practically possible. Many such businesses resort to raising money from friends and family since it is the easiest, quickest and the least expensive form of financing. It is wise to raise capital in smaller chunks from different friends and family sources so that you don't run the risk of ruining the relationship in case your business fails. The cost of capital in the case of raising money from friends or family could below. Still, the emotional costs associated with the relationship could be high, especially when the business has a downturn, and you are not able to repay the money that you've taken.

- **Lenders:** Lenders would require a fully complete business plan before they lend money to you. As lenders, they are primarily interested in your projected cash flows, since they want to know if you will generate sufficient cash flows to repay the loan along with the interest. Borrowing money comes with a cost – the interest that you need to pay, and the loan documentation and other applicable fees. Many lenders require a personal guarantee or collateral to ensure that the loan is secure.

- **Equity Investors:** In the world of equity investors, several players are willing to take a bet on your business and invest capital. The earliest stage investors are called angel investors. Consider these investors as angels who invest money in early-stage start-ups and businesses where there is no history of earnings. Many angels would also offer mentoring advise entrepreneurs.

Coverage of a Good Business Plan

A good business plan will explain your business goals and will layout the future roadmap of your business. A business plan usually covers the following sections:

- **Executive Summary:** An executive summary is the thesis statement of your business plan. It is usually written after the entire business plan has been completed. The executive summary summarizes who you are, what your business does, where your business is headed, how you are managing your cash flows, and what your exit strategy will be. The executive summary should address the 5W1H formula – What? Where? Why? Who? When? And How?

- **Business Summary:** The first major section of the business plan is the business summary that addresses the organizational details of your business. Start the business summary with a brief description of your business, what you intend doing, and the products/services that you are selling. While writing this section you need to understand your vision of the business – what you want to accomplish and determine the strategy that you will deploy to help the business reach its short-term and long-term goals.

- **Products and Services:** In this section, you will describe the products and services that you are selling. Is there a real need for your product or service? How is your product or service solving a problem, and how will it be different from the ones existing in the market? Give photographs of your primary product categories in this section. If you have plans to launch a set of products or product lines in the future, this is the place to describe them.

- **Market Research:** The market section of the business plan defines all aspects of your target market and your marketing strategy. The market research should discuss the market size, trends, demographics, target market, and your marketing strategy (both online and offline) to capture your target market. Market research can prevent your company from making erroneous decisions that result in expensive design mistakes in new products, and marketing campaigns.

- **Operational Plan:** In this section of the business plan, you will have to discuss how the business is put together from a functional perspective. Keep in mind, as you write this section of the business plan, you will have to include the necessary elements of revenues and costs in the financial section of the business plan.

- **Financial Plan:** The financial section of the business plan shows the past (in case you are an existing business), current and the future projected finances. In this section, you will have to discuss the financial ask (i.e. the amount of capital that you are raising by way of loan or equity), the projected income statements, cash flows and balance sheets.

Financing your Business

When you are starting a new business or expanding your current operations, you will have to answer the following questions:

- How much money do I need?

- Will I need to raise capital from external sources?

- What are the sources available?

- How much will it cost me?

The first step in financing your business is to assess how much capital you will need to run your business. In assessing the amount of capital that you would need for your business, you will have to identify the major costs, sources of revenue and the risks associated with the business itself.

Once you have decided on the capital that you require, you will need to carefully determine the amount you need, and when you will need it. Many entrepreneurs make the grave mistake of overestimating or underestimating the capital requirements – both of which could lead to serious problems. It is for this reason that you need a realistic business plan with conservative assumptions, that covers all areas of your business idea.

After you have decided to raise capital, the next step is to identify the sources of raising capital. There are two broad sources from which you can raise capital – debt and equity.

Debt Capital

Debt capital is generally obtained from two broad sources. It could come from a non-professional source like a friend, relative or a collage, or a traditional lending institution like a bank, a venture debt company, or directly from the Small Business Administration (SBA).

- **Family and Friends:** The most common and readily available source are from family and friends when the capital requirements are smaller. This is usually the cheapest form of debt financing available but could put the personal relationships at risk when things go bad.

- **Angels:** Angel investors are usually successful business people, who have a high net worth, and are typically willing to invest up to $500,000. A good source of finding such angels is through business associations such as the local chamber of commerce. There are also many angel investment-groups where investors form a syndicate (like a fund) to invest in businesses. Angel investors pool in money into the syndicate, which in turn invests in businesses. A professional management team manages these syndicates. Some of the top angel investor networks are:

  - Astia Angels
  - Band of Angels

- Bay Angels

- Broadway Angels

- Golden Seeds

- Investor's Circle

- J-Angels

- Keiretsu Forum

- Life Science Angels

- MIT Alumni Angels of Northern California

- North Bay Angels

- Oxford Angel Fund

- Rubicon Venture Capital

- Sand Hill Angels

- The Angels Forum

- TiE Angels

- US Angel Investors

- Wharton Alumni Angels

- **Banks:** Traditional bands and lenders have been a major source of business finance. Most of these banks are strict about the collateral requirements, especially post-2008 crisis. Some of the banks and lenders also require the owner to inject a portion of the funding requirement as equity, which could typically range from 10% to 50% of the total funding requirements.

- **SBA Guaranteed Loans:** The SBA guarantee program offers a secondary source of financing where entrepreneurs are unable to raise capital from private lending sources. Most of the SBA loans are made by private lenders but are backed by an SBA guarantee. The SBA loans are focused on small businesses and often provide better repayment terms and interest rates.

Equity Capital

If your business already has a loan or is ineligible for getting a loan from any of the sources listed above, then you will probably need to seek equity investments. Equity capital usually comes from the following sources:

- **Friends and Family:** Friends and family are often the most sought-after source for finding equity investments early on. As discussed earlier, these could cause a strain on personal relationships if the business takes a downturn.

- **SBA Licensed Investment Companies:** The SBA licenses Small Business Investment Companies (SBICs). These companies make equity investments into small companies under various schemes and programs. SBICs invest in small companies in exchange for an ownership interest. The investment usually ranges from $100,000 to $5 million. To apply for investment from SBIC, you should be a U.S. small business. You should be operating in an approved industry (Businesses like farmland and real estate don't qualify for investment under SBIC).

- **Professional Investors:** Professional investors usually venture capitalists or private equity firms. They take a risk by investing in businesses and expect the highest return as compared to most other sources of funding. To get funding from professional investors your business has to have a clear exit strategy and be highly scalable.

- **Crowdfunding:** Crowdfunding is the practice of funding your business by raising small amounts of capital from a large number of investors, typically through the internet. Some of the most famous crowdfunding websites are:

- Kickstarter
- GoFundMe
- Indiegogo
- Patreon
- RocketHub

Indicative Business Plan Checklist

A good business plan contains the five major sections and an annex where all the supporting documents are attached. Given below is an indicative checklist of what you will have to cover in your business plan:

Section 1: The Executive Summary Checklist

As discussed earlier, the executive summary is a summary of your business plan. The general rule of thumb is that the executive summary should be as short and crisp as possible and should not exceed two pages. The executive summary

should typically answer the following questions:

- What is the problem that you are solving?

- What is your solution?

- Who is your target market?

- What are the market dynamics – market size, trends,

  demographics?

- Is there existing competition?

- How is the solution different from that of the

  competitors?

- How much capital are you seeking to raise?

- What will be the uses of the capital that you are

  raising?

- Who will be owning and managing the business?

- What is their experience relevant to the business

  model?

- How will the business generate revenues and cash flows?

- What are the major financial indicators of the business for the next 3-5 years?

- What is the implementation plan – What is the schedule of short-term and long-term milestones that the business is going to achieve?

Specific questions that need to be addressed:

- Lender:

  - When will the loan be repaid?

  - What collateral or guarantee will be provided for the loan?

  - Is there any interest moratorium or holiday that you are seeking?

- Equity:

  - What will be the value proposition of the business?

  - What is your exit strategy?

  - What are the returns that you likely to give to investors?

Section 2: Business Summary Checklist

In this section, you will discuss your business, what it does, the products and services, and give a broad overview of the nature of your business. The business summary section should answer the following questions:

- What is the name of your business?

- When was it established?

- What is the legal structure (LLC, S-Corp, C-Corp?)

- Who owns the business?

- Where will the business be located?

- What are the main products and services that the business sells?

- What is your mission?

- What are your short-term goals?

- Do you have any strategic relationships? How will they benefit the company?

- Do you have a proprietary product/technology?

- Do you have any unique business model?

Section 3: Products and Services Checklist

In this section, you will outline the major products and services that your business is going to sell. You will have to answer the following questions:

- Manufacturers
  - What are the major products that you are going to sell?
  - What is the manufacturing process?

228

- What are the stages of research and development?

- What are the raw materials that are used in production?

- Are your raw materials available?

- Who are your major suppliers?

- Where are they located?

- Why did you choose them?

- Are there any alternative suppliers?

- How can you address a sudden surge in the orders?

- Who will distribute your products?

- Retailers

  - What are the major products that you are going to sell?

  - How will you procure them?

  - Who are the major vendors?

- What are the terms with the vendors?

- What is your system for managing and tracking inventory?

- How do you determine the volume of goods?

- What are your sales channels – online? Amazon, Walmart?

- Service Providers

  - What is the service that you are providing?

  - How will the service be different from that of the competitors?

  - What resources do you require to provide the service?

Section 4: Market Research Checklist

This section requires an in-depth market research. Your marketing strategy will be a key tool in helping your business achieve its goals and objectives. You will have to answer the following questions:

- What is the market that you are trying to address?
- What are the market dynamics – size, trends, growth?
- What are the different market segments in your market?
- What is your target market segment?
- What is your ideal buyer's persona?
- What are the key drivers of demand?
- What are the local market trends in the geographies where you intend to sell your product or service?
- What do you hope to accomplish through your marketing strategy? What are your marketing goals?
- Do you have a clear branding strategy? What is the current level of brand awareness for your company/product/service?

- Who are your best customers?

- What is their buying pattern?

- What are their income levels?

- What are their age and other demographics?

- How can you reach your customers, online and offline?

- What particular characteristic in your company/product/service will bring loyal customers back to you?

- What is your customer acquisition strategy?

- What is your customer retention strategy?

- What is the Cost of Acquiring a Customer (CAC)?

- How long do you anticipate your customers to use your product? What is the Customer Lifetime Value (LTV)?

- What new level of sales can your business handle?

- What quantities of your product/service can you sell? What are the constraints and how does your business plan address these constraints?

- Who is competing with you? What are their strengths and weaknesses?

- What weaknesses of your competitors can you capitalize?

- How is your company/product/service different from that of the competitors?

- What is your pricing strategy?

- How does your pricing compare to that of the competitors?

- What is your competitive pricing when it comes to pricing?

- Do you need to address your pricing when a competitor makes a change?

- What are your sales channels?

- Do you have trained sales team and sales materials to kick-start your sales process?

- What incentives are you giving your sales staff, and partners to market and sell your product?

- Is your website ready?

- Has the website been optimized for SEO?

- Do you have social media handles?

- Are you considering social media marketing in your marketing strategy?

- What is your advertising strategy – both online and offline?

- Do you have a clear public relations strategy in place?

- Does your product/service require after-sales support?

- If yes, what is your customer service policy and process?

- Who will be responsible for implementing your marketing strategy?

- Are you outsourcing any of the marketing functions? If yes, to whom and what are the cost implications?

Section 5: Operational Plan Checklist

In this section of the business plan, you will have to cover how your business functions from an operations perspective. You will have to answer the following questions:

- Where will your business be located? Include a picture of the layouts, maps, and floor plans.

- Will the premise be owned or leased?

- What are the expected annual rental costs?

- What are the channels of sale?

- What is your legal structure?

- Who are the owners and corporate officers of the business?

- Do you anticipate changes in the legal structure in the future? If yes, when and why?

- Who is going to manage the business?

- What are their educational qualifications and experience relevant to the business?

- What are the key strengths and weaknesses of the management team?

- Who will be your team of advisors and accountants?

- What will be the organizational structure? Who will be reporting to whom?

- What are the key skills that you require to run your business?

- What is the staffing plan for the next 3-5 years?

- What is your hiring policy, and annual appraisal policy?

- What are the job descriptions of the various staff that you are planning to recruit in the staffing plan?

- How will the staff be compensated: salaries, bonuses, stock options, benefits, vacations?

- What are the key training requirements? How will you ensure that your staff will be trained on the job requirements?

- What accounting system will you use in your business?

- Who will be responsible for the reliability and efficiency of the accounting information?

- Will you be using an outside accountant?

- Who will be doing the business taxes?

- What are the annual compliance and regulatory requirements for your business?

- Does the business need any licenses to operate? If yes, what is the status of the licenses that are required to be obtained?

- Who will take care of the legal requirements of the firm?

- In case of a lawsuit, do you have an attorney to help you defend the lawsuit?

- What are the intellectual properties that are available to the business?

- What kinds of insurance does your business require?

- Apart from the usual fire and marine insurance, do you have insurance specific to your business – product liability, professional indemnity?

- What is the security policy for your company? How do you ensure that key assets of your business (including technical know-how, patents) are not stolen?

- Are any of your products or processes or technology patentable? If yes, what is the stage of getting them patented?

Section 6: Financial Plan

In this section of the business plan, you are required to outline the financial aspects of your business. Try to be as realistic as possible – do not overstate your revenues or understate your expenses. You will have to answer the following questions:

- Sources and Uses of Funds
    - How much capital are you intending to raise?
    - How much of that will be through a loan, and how much will be equity?
    - What are the terms of the loan? (interest, repayment, other terms)
    - How will the capital be used?
    - Have you obtained quotations from reputed vendors?

- What are the key assumptions based on which you have arrived at the usage of funds?

- Have you considered contingencies and working capital?

- Income Statements

  - What are the key sources of revenue for the business?

  - What are the expected selling prices for each of these revenue channels?

  - What are the volumes projected for each of these channels/products/services?

  - What is the expected increase in revenue, and what is your expected market share?

  - What are your major costs?

  - How are these costs increasing over a period of time?

- What is the inflation level that you've assumed in the cost structure?

- What are the key revenue and cost drivers?

- What are your Earnings Before Interest, Tax, Depreciation and Amortization (EBITDA)?

- How does your cost structure benchmark with your competitors and industry data?

- What are the key sensitive assumptions that could change your projections?

- Have you considered sales tax and income tax in your projections?

- What are the fixed costs and variable costs in your business?

- What is the breakeven point, and in which year do you achieve breakeven?

- Do you have a monthly projection for the next 24 months?

- In case of an existing business, is your projected income statement in line with your business' past? If not, why?

- Working Capital
  - What is the receivable cycle in your business? What credit terms do you offer?
  - What are the inventory requirements for your business?
  - How many days of inventory are you normally required to hold?
  - What are the payment terms negotiated with your suppliers?
  - What are the expected levels of current assets?
  - What are the expected levels of current liabilities?

- What is the gross working capital requirement of the business?
- How will this working capital requirement be funded?
- Have you considered this working capital in the sources and uses of funds?
- Do you have a monthly projection for the next 24 months?

- Cash Flows
  - What are the sources of cash inflow and cash outflow?
  - When does your business turn cash-positive?
  - What are the funding requirements based on the cash flows that you've projected?
  - What are the long-term assets that you require in your business?

- What is your annual capital expenditure (Capex) requirements?

- If you are taking out a loan, do you have sufficient cash to repay your loan along with interest?

- Does your business have sufficient cash flows and potential for growth, that might interest a venture capitalist?

- Do you have a monthly projection for the next 24 months?

- Ratios and Analysis

  - Have you performed a ratio analysis?

  - Have you benchmarked your business ratios with that of the competitors and the industry as a whole?

- Have you performed a vertical financial statement analysis (also known as the common sized analysis)?

- Lender Specific Requirements
  - Does your business have sufficient cash flows to repay the loan?
  - What is your interest service coverage ratio, and debt-service coverage ratio?

- Investors Specific Requirements
  - Is the projected growth attractive to prospective investors?
  - Does the projected growth go hand in hand with your exit strategy?
  - Have you considered stock dividends in your cash flows?

Annex to the Business Plan

In the annex to the business plan, you will provide all the supporting documents that are necessary to back up the statements made in the main business plan. You will have to include the following:

- Management resumes and profiles
- Owner's financial statements
- Credit reports (if you are approaching a lender)
- Lease documents
- Detailed findings of the market research (surveys, questionnaires)
- Articles of incorporation or operating agreements
- DBAs
- Business licenses
- Copyrights, trademarks, patents
- Insurance policies
- Licensing agreements

- Major contracts

- Vendor agreements

Chapter 8

Broken or Broken Open

A Sound Way Forward

The year 2020 will be a radical moment of great change. Even more so than after the Great Recession of 2008, it harkens for a real call to action from all aspects of society. It is a time of great historical significance with the catastrophic upheaval from the pandemic, and now the Black Lives Matter movement which has turned into a full-blown civil rights movement. We are heading toward one of the most controversial elections in modern times, and there are seismic shifts in the global power structure. My last book was a wake-up call for many of my colleagues who own and operate a small business. This book was written to address the very nature of business. Continual challenges and the existential threat brought on by the pandemic has once again accelerated the need to harness technology just like our large business counterparts. If you are in survival mode, you can derive some comfort in the fact that it is again not a result of your own negligence. So many of us, as owners, blame ourselves and feel like such losers, that we should have known and planned for such catastrophic losses. How could we have known that such a devastating health crisis would have spread around the world in a matter of a few months? With a record, unemployment predicted to reach 30%, greater than The Great Depression at 24.9% and not only that, in the middle of all this, George Floyd was murdered and the outcry on the streets is something never seen before anywhere in the world.

Will all this change the image of Brand America forever? The old image of America is why businesses want to start here because of the well-branded security of our free markets. We need to restore this sensibility before it is too late, and the injury to the American Brand is tarnished and irrevocably lost to countries like Finland, Switzerland, Sweden, Belgium, Luxembourg, Norway, Canada, The Netherlands, Japan, and Denmark, as rated in The world Economic Forums inaugural report in 2020, a list based on education, healthcare, economic dynamism, quality of life, political environment and social protections. Conspicuously low in the ranking is the United States. The United States received a 27, but this ranking may have gone down since the exposure of the Black Lives Matter Movement exploded after the murder by police of George Floyd. Even now, touting that America is the greatest nation in the world is less believable around the world and to its own citizens.[cxxi]

In my first book, I had to use research to explain why small businesses were at the breaking point. In this edition, it is clear that the unprecedented public health crisis, social isolation and lockdowns of all businesses accept essential institutions and companies has created a situation of the most direr circumstances. The shocking thing is that there are 47.7 million of us and we comprise 99.9 percent of all businesses. Our influence and impact are reflected in our numbers. As a collective group, potentially, this is a large coalition. It is also clear that our customer base is mostly gone and that the nature of our large consuming population has changed at least for a decade. Literally, there is very little money circulating and fewer people spending on what is available. So how do we move this barometer? How do we find more customers? How do we change this downward trajectory fast and," back to that "shining city on the hill"?

We Must Go it Alone with Cooperation and Creativity!
This country was founded, not just by people, but founded by an ideal. At the center of these ideals was freedom. In

the past five years, minority-owned businesses have

increased by 400 percent, while non-minority businesses

only grew by 6 percent. There is no greater sense of

freedom than working for yourself. So, the trend is clear the

road to more wealth and equality is that these businesses

have to work hard to save themselves during this crisis, or

they could turn back decades of progress. Americans

commonly regard their society as the freest and the best in

the world. Most of our ancestors came across the oceans

with very little, longing for this freedom in a land of new,

open opportunities. Basically, we are a nation populated by

immigrants who came here to work hard for a better life.

The American ideal of freedom is that all people are

created equal and that the role of government is to protect

each person's basic rights.[cxxii]

The disparity in income, the lack of a level playing field in

our market place, and the selling out by our elected

officials and public servants are what we need to work together to change and to resolve. The systemic racism of so much of our institutions must be eradicated. If so, it could unlock so many talented entrepreneurs. It is a priority in our hierarchy of needs right now, as many of us are in survival mode. Still, we are also in a turning point in our demand for equal rights under the law for blacks, minorities and women and the LGBTQ communities in America. We cannot deal with these pervasive issues later. The time has come to deal with these inequalities while we are experiencing quantum changes in all aspects of our society. We must work to make our companies healthier, and we can work together to force the changes that will benefit the country and small businesses because we are the majority.

The top one percent has a better chance of making it than the rest of us. Good for them! Perhaps this group was smarter and stronger than the rest of us, but not for long.

Out of our own instinct for survival, it is evident that to win against a larger competitor; we need to work together. There is strength in numbers.

We are all sick of watching political theatre when our businesses and security for a better life is in jeopardy. Worse still is what are our children going to think of us when we leave them with the burden of all that crushing debt and nowhere to turn to earn that money. The US Treasury's official figure for the **debt** of the **United States government** on May 21, 2020, is $25.5 trillion—or more precisely—$25,466,764,338,935. This amounts to $77,268 for every **person** living in the United States and $198,063 for every household.[cxxiii]

We have strayed from our ideals, and now we see what we have netted unless we turn back the clock to what we know are true American values. Directly associated with our value of freedom is the ideal of progress. The desire to progress by making use of opportunities is essential to Americans. Many Americans can boost that with each succeeding generation, the family's status has improved because they came to America. The classic American family saga is all about progress. The great-grandparents arriving from the old world with nothing, suffer poverty and working hard so that they can provide a good education for their children. These ideals are then past down to proceeding generations. Through our families and in our schools, we are taught to believe in these ideals that anyone can live a good life and their dreams can be achieved by hard work, family loyalty, and faith in the free enterprise system. We see that this progress or progression has changed radically.[cxxiv]

Unfortunately, reality has taught us a lesson; that the American dream is not open to everybody and that our

Representatives favor those who help him/her get re-elected. The same exact lobbyist influences both political parties; it is absurd. So, on the same issues like Fanny and Freddy, Dodd-Frank, Deregulation, Repeal of Glass Segal, the Debt Ceiling and all the so-called preeminent issues of the day both parties had their hand in the cookie jar. That the causes of this finance dysfunction are clearly the product of both parties ineptitude and overriding influence of Special interests. How can any of us really know who is at fault and certainly how it can be corrected because there are so many complex convoluting issues that confound what is really basic arithmetic? With so much divisiveness, we are acting out but not acting in our own best interest. Unless we work together, there is no way out not for individuals or for entire country.

With a newly found creativity to spin the issues in favor of one political party or the other, it makes it next to impossible to evaluate who is right or wrong. And we talk about this openly, and the hypocrisy keeps poll figures for Congress at a record low of 25 percent. It almost seems by keeping this confusion going it gives special interest a way to get in front of the passing or not passing of most policy bills. There is no truth anymore.

Change of Attitude is the Answer Because Small Business Owners Have the Grit and the Guts to Make It Happen

What has been an effective tool in the past, and one that can be even more effective in the future because of technology is forming a group, a network, a coalition, a team of like minds who believe in the same goals and objectives and that within this group you can effect change in a big way. It is here that leaderless we can confront our demons and utilize all of our much-needed resources to figure out our own economy. We are on our own anyway!

Small business owners are a unique breed of American because it takes grit and guts to start and run a business. In today's world, it takes the heart of a Marine (whether male or female) to face the battles of each passing day. When a business goes into survival mode, it becomes a very stressful way of life. For many of us worrying about making payroll each week, paying our suppliers, reinventing yourself in a retailesque environment every day is a ride down a rollercoaster most months. And, when there is blood in the market because most businesses were forced to close and can only re-open and serve 25 percent of their potential customers because of social distancing requirements. Large companies who have no problem retooling are vicious competitors and so can your customers will be eminently more aggressive about price and value because they are going through the same economic distress or joblessness. When you own and operate a business that is not profitable, and each day brings the challenges of sales, personnel, marketing, finance, one can get demoralized rather quickly.

I never served in the Marines, but I am sure for many of us, it feels like we are going into battle every day in these dysfunctional economic times. We all forge ahead because we must. As small business owners, we never ask for a handout. Small companies do not have banking relationships so that most larger concerns were able to benefit from the CARES ACT. Perhaps that is why there are few or no government programs that will really benefit small businesses that are holding on.

I have made a study of all the viable programs available for small businesses; these are all listed, linked and summarized on the Business SOS™ website. There are approximately 470 Federally funded offices to service the needs of 47.7 million companies, a relatively poor network of resources for such a large country. I do believe it is a direct result of our belief in the free enterprise system and a prevailing attitude of business owners that we are in it on our own. Just leave us alone, and we can make it happen. The unfortunate reality is that success, as the economic cards show, currently, is stacked against us. The complexities of all the mitigating factors make these changes next to impossible for many of us.

Business SOS™ is not a response to businesses needing a free handout because we do not. Business SOS™ is a place where business owners can finally acquire information about existing programs and what they can and cannot really do for them without wasting precious time. It is also a place where we can get help or help your neighbor.

Do You Need to Send an SOS?

What do I mean exactly? Business SOS™ will function as a network of businesses in four ways. First, and foremost: if you are a business in distress, we are committed to helping you get whatever you need to resuscitate your business if it is still a viable business model for the 21st Century and post COVID-19 Business environment. On the website, all you need to do is scroll over the SOS symbol. This will immediately enable you to make contact with us. There will be an SOS hotline as well. Here we outline our commitment to the distressed small business, the first being the most important, which is confidentiality. As I mentioned before, addressing this problem has been difficult because of the consequences that could result in competitors or employees learning about the distress of your company. Hence, we have outlined that unless authorized; otherwise, the SOS business has our complete confidentiality. Except, of course, to discuss and connect to relevant resources that could assist this small business. It is also not a bait-and-switch, where the distressed business is asked to join with undisclosed or additional cost. It is a true resource for businesses to gain the help they need when they need it. At first, we will rely on each community. Later, we plan to go national, and we will connect with other businesses that are willing to help in the areas most necessary.

Sponsors

Hence, we are looking for small and large businesses that have embraced our old fashioned American ideal of helping our neighbor. Still, because of the digital age, they may be located in your city or region, or perhaps a crossed the country. It is a powerful, timely call to action to help your colleagues and in turn, help yourself. It is to provoke action and progress, which is vital to changing the negative trends we are now entangled. What does a sponsor gain from his benevolence? The sponsor gains invaluable internal and external PR. PR not in the commercial sense but in the true value of the great moment in time we are all a part of, and the good feeling of helping your fellow American out of his distress and in turn helping yourself and your country.

Sponsors are companies that have the knowhow, technology, financial acumen, services, human resources, construction for modern physical plants, communication equipment, smart machines, green technology, marketing, transactions, legal, quality control, equipment, transportation, production of all types of products and services, experts in various field. Business SOS™ will provide each company in SOS access to a variety of companies that have signed on to provide real help not just advice to our struggling small business neighbor.

Our Volunteers

Volunteers will be another primary aspect of Business SOS™ because not all members will be owners or operators of a business that can provide direct retooling or service to our struggling businesses some will come from organizations with specific expertise. Individuals that have worked in various aspects or key disciplines that can assist our businesses in ways to rectify areas that are critical for our businesses to pull themselves out of survival mode and into a thriving mode for the challenges ahead.

This type of network developed at the grassroots level in every one of our communities can effectively change the course of events by helping each individual business to regain control but also put control back in the hands of the people who are willing to make these important attitude changes for themselves and their country.

**Let's Accept the Hard Work and Pain in Order to Get
Back Our Country**

I always told my staff that control is freedom and freedom is happiness a very simple equation. With the lack of leadership in Washington and their obvious inability to enact policy that makes sense, it is imperative that we get our small businesses functioning and producing so that we can pay the taxes that are needed to pay for our city and state service and educate our children and pay down this debt. It sounds painful, but how about it is also the noble thing to do. And probably the only way out of this mess for enough companies.

We all do it every day when we sit down and develop our own budgets. No thinking person would run up their debt so destructively as our government and large banks have done in order to give more tax breaks to the rich. In fact, it is not brain surgery what Washington needs to do; they just won't because it does not serve the purpose of the people or

corporations that gain the most from all of this confusion

and have rustled control of our markets out of the larger

body of taxpayers and into the hands of the one percent

who convinced you they were paying all the taxes and

creating all the jobs.

Small Business Hiring Powers Recovery...

**Share of Net Job Creation Since the End of
the Downturn by Employment Size of Firm**

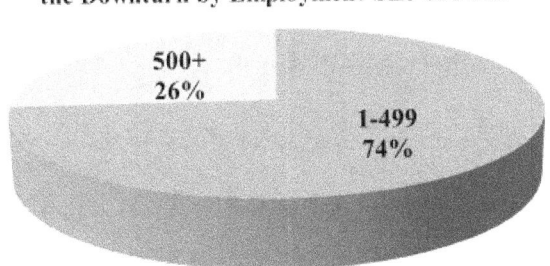

Source: ADP National Employment Report.

cxxv

Small businesses are creating the largest portion of the jobs

in American, and with this newfound energy could create

an even greater amount than ever before.

Business SOS™ is for all of those companies and committed Americans who are proud to play by the rules of fairness because those rules do work. As we watch all of this lack of transparency and accountability, in the end, we will all lose… even the one-percenters. Bad ethics drives good ethics out,[cxxvi] but we are determined to set the example of what being a true American is really about.

It is all about real progress because that matters to us and is a pivotal part of our ideals. We want to work hard and get scrappy to do the little things that will make a difference. None of us needs government help because we can and will help ourselves? We can rely on our team of small businesses to be there and help each one of us figure it out and then to be there to support us for the long hall.

I am sure all of us have supported a friend or a relative when they started businesses by offering advice, and going in and just buying whatever it is they have to sell. That attitude of a community must be resuscitated. The pride in our hard work and the ethics to produce high-quality products and services are so important and must be restored. We have learned a dreadful lesson about placing all of our essential product production off-shore. For years we have cried for all of that big business liquidity to invest that money back home. But they did not! All the companies did with those large tax breaks are to buy back stock so that the value of their stock was enriched. It did not trickle down.

Bring Back American, Made in a Big Way

I am in Miami, and so many Cuban Americans envied American ingenuity, "American Made" that label meant something. Things were not made of plastic; they were made with stainless steel. There is real brand equity that we forge during our counties growth to foster and establish American products as having a higher quality standard than most countries. This was born out of our ideals we have been discussing where products were made with integrity. We are all aware that American manufacturing must be on the rise in this post-COVID-19 phase. This is a point of departure for many companies to examine the viability of returning to the homeland instead of outsourcing jobs overseas when the quality standards just cannot compare. I do not want to jump on any China bandwagon, but it does seem that they purposely hid the human to a human transmission issue with the WHO. However, it would not be smart until we are in a better financial position to create a cold war with the second-largest economy. For years the situation has vastly changed from the '90s when labor in China was cheap. We have been writing about this for years, and in an article in Wired Magazine, Brenda Koenner[cxxvii] states that "one reason to abandon China is quality: some products are too flawed to sell." For many US firms, the decision to manufacture overseas is a no-brainer. Labor costs in China and other developing nations have been so low that as recently as two or three years ago, anyone who refused to was viewed as a dinosaur. But China now has seen a rise in wages and demands from their own workforce, so the bargain it once was is now up for serious evaluation. For the small business that makes up the largest sector of innovators in the US, it is time to rethink this businesses model of taking their production and supply chain to the other side of the world. But retooling is costly. How do these companies find the manufacturing facilities here in the US or capitalize their own businesses for this production? Business SOS™ wants to fill this gap at a rapid pace by integrating our sponsors and members.[cxxviii]

Wal-Marts and other big monopolies need to be busted up in order for the country to get back to the new normal. Wal-Mart is the ultimate offender. It is a known fact of economics that you do not import more than you can export. Realizing that all of our officials in Washington may not be educated in the more complex issues within the discipline of economics, but, surely, they are aware of these basic facts. Yet when examining all of the trade bills passed in the last 30 years, it is evident that lobbyist had their hand in blinding our officials into ignoring these basic premises. Despite this error, we can change that equation by developing trade to suit the purpose of our small businesses.

We Need to Create a Real Call-to-Action

In my first book, I clearly outline my failures and how the boom-bust economy had taken me by surprise. This is a whole new set of circumstance. This is the perfect storm of economic crisis as I outlined in chapter 1. But many experts in business will say that the longer we are closed, the harder it will be to get back. Not only will our workers lose their skills but starting an economy as large as the US will take serious action. Right now, the powers in Washington seem to think it is spending more of our children's future. I disagree. Having started over several times from nothing and knowing hundreds of entrepreneurs who also started with nothing I simply think with the right game plan any company can rethink their products and services or perhaps abandon them completely and start anew. We have to be focused on what is currently in demand and what will be the demand post-COVID-19. It is now time to work and learn for free. Yes, I said that because I am willing to do that myself if it means I can help someone or learn a new skill. It is time to go to companies you know can help you and ask them to work with you until your concepts take hold. Be conscious of your daily contribution to your business and other local businesses around you because your country needs to see an uptick in productivity. If you do a study on the search term motivation. America ranks last in Google search. No one is interested in the term perhaps because no one is motivated to know more about it. We need to buckle down and change our attitude and get energized. What better way than to help your neighbor and your country to break this terrible downward curve?

How Do We Take Advantage of Technology to Sell and Gain Larger Markets?

These are the most unusual times. Keeping a distance from one another will affect businesses for the next two years. So, the only way we can communicate and expand our markets is through technology. The problem there is that many small business owners do not know how to enact these changes. It is complicated. It is also costly to keep these new systems working and reporting and keeping up with changes that will continue to occur. In my first book, I revealed how inadequate I was in the retooling of my business. This resistance was my downfall. Please listen to what I am saying here. I believe that we are not Broken, but these challenges will leave up broken-open to new ways of operation. Each aspect I discuss here from creativity to collective thinking and integration with other companies is what will and can work. This integration is what we are striving for with Business SOS™, which makes this method an option that will help specific small businesses find new customers or new resources enabling them to get out of this trend of bankruptcy or just surviving.

It is important that just like other fragile concepts like Democracy it takes vigilance to keep it secure from degradation, this too applies to our approach to reopening our businesses. What would America look like if our Representatives today truly looked out for the benefit of small businesses and not just Wall Street? Notice how Wall Street suffer losses at the beginning of COVID-19 but now seems to be just fine. Well, our Treasury printed enough money and threw enough capital to keep these big companies solid. We all are cognizant that the corner store was not essential when but conglomerates like Wall-mart were able to continue making money? This is not a pity party but a chance to wake up and help each other one company at a time.

Ignite Small Businesses and a Renewed Sense of Hope

"The more that the dysfunction of the human mind plays itself out on the world stage, clearly visible to everyone in the daily television news reports, the greater the number of people who realize the urgent need for a radical change in human consciousness if humanity is not to destroy both itself and the planet."[cxxix]

I closed my last book with this powerful quote from Tolle. During each economic challenge, the message is the same. This holds true with all of the health financial and social protections that are now at stake in this volatile world we are living each day. Similar to the enlightened teachings of this spiritual Guru I found it once again imperative to expose the true state of America's small businesses and the resistance to what Tolle calls the "suchness" of the present moment. At times I am certain the information seems harsh, cynical or much too complicated and difficult to face. Unfortunately, it is the only way toward creating understanding, knowledge and consciousness that fits the reality of our times and creates the dissatisfaction in critical mass that brings about the kind of change significant enough to matter to such a large body of businesses and people. Look at all the protests not just here but all over the world.

This Collective Gestalt could foster the dynamic thinking transformative enough to move many millions of people and economic equality forward at the same time. If we all jumped in together as a proactive network and inclusively opened sourced all of our resources with the right tools, creative thinking and a willingness to work together utilizing all of the benefits of the digital age and the opportunity to work all a crossed the globe we can be successful. If we all surrender as Tolle discusses to the possibilities that are "now" that our mutual efforts would achieve together, it could be a renaissance of sorts for a new kind of world and entrepreneurship. It is very exciting, uplifting and offers hope to so many.

Human consciousness, whether it is spiritual or societal is the same transformative process that Tolle offers in our desire to evolve into something or someone better. It is the same passion and excitement, which manifested in the enlightened thinkers who fought for our liberty or wrote our Constitution to create the Greatest Republic on earth. It is what galvanized the abolitionist, suffragettes, and now hundreds of thousands of protesters on the streets of

America in an unprecedented plea for fairness. We have been inspired by freedom riders and gay activists who were successful in their movements for change. The vast inequality of our system as it stands now must go. It is the social imperative of our time. I focus here on this manuscript on small businesses, but we all know that the times will dictate massive changes far beyond those I discuss here for small businesses.

True knowledge or consciousness about the dysfunctional economy that many of us are now suffering allows one to recognize what is false and faulty with clarity. This awakening to bring us to a collective "big thinking and collaboration" is part of our culture and history as a country that responds to the needs of its people.

This transformation in the way we compete, collaborate and communicate is not in the distant future but here now

as Tolle reiterates about spiritualism. It is available NOW-
no matter who or where you are. Being proud of what you
are doing as an individual person or business and how you
are affecting others can create a new American patriotism if
enough individuals and businesses speak out, which is
finally happening before our very eyes.

Change is difficult and frightening. It connotates in some
instances, defeat, giving up, failing to rise to the challenges
of life or the times. It is so difficult that it sometimes does
not occur unless there is a major catastrophe like COVID-
19 or grave injustice as in the case of George Floyd and
dozens of other black and brown individuals who have to
long suffer racism. I am again changing, but this time I am
prepared because of the massive failures, I went through in
the last debacle in 2008. This time I approach the current
climate with skills and confidence, I did not have before,
and I am ready willing and able to show other people and

companies the way forward. In my instance, it was the death of my business that had been successful for so long that it became a part of my identity, power and social standing. I have matured and could care less about those things any more. I care about my small business brothers and sisters because I know what works.

It is always a difficult process to reveal openly my failures and the true state of my once very successful business, but now I have done it again and want to share my knowledge. I also realize it was not just me, but millions of small businesses a crossed the country in 2008, and now in 2020 it is the entire economic foundation of the United States that is in jeopardy.

To watch your business slowly die or disintegrate is very distressing for all of us. For a long time, I had an unwillingness to accept it and was very unhappy and depressed that I could not rebuild. I was immobilized with shock and fear. I became listless, lethargic and angry, which is totally unlike me as I have always had an intense energy level and a positive attitude toward life as many self-made entrepreneurs do. We are a group of highly motivated individuals with unique skills. But this has been a challenge bigger and deeper than most of us are able to wrap our arms around. The last crisis I was able to rebuild again from nothing, and this time I will help others with the skills I have learned through all the hell I went through. I was able to save my own business so close to destruction, and I am able to retool for the challenges ahead with this new crisis.

I utilized all of the concepts I discussed in these pages, such as partnerships and teaming, marketing on all three screens and expanded my operation, utilizing all three screens to advance inbound client response. Business SOS™ is my activist component to my marketing agency, and it allows me to pay forward to my colleagues and country that I feel I have an obligation as a fellow citizen to care about and assist. I am not in it alone as we have learned. This is why I am developing as we speak the proprietary software capable of bringing struggling businesses, Sponsors, Volunteers, experts and other Guru's together to bring to bare all of the assets, strengths and expertise and potential to help each other out of this pervasive mess.

The goal is that Business SOS™ will provide the assistance, knowledge, and tooling to compete in a larger business arena against all the new and unforeseen mitigating forces currently affecting our economy. Business SOS™ will help small businesses level the playing field. The small business will achieve integration and will be allowed into the opportunities of the 21st Century through the help of their neighbor and community, which are the original American values. These values are as old as the very first settlers who conquered the challenges of the 17th, 18th, 19th and 20th Centuries. By helping each other, we help ourselves, take on big challenges together. Business SOS™ is only the vehicle it is the "power of now" that will ignite the momentum.

Chapter one gave you a complete outline of the true state of our small businesses today. This is not a panacea; there are pockets of industries that are still feeling no pain. However, the vast majority feels it and fears it every day waiting for the other economic shoe to drop. This is an unsettling feeling when our family's lives are at stake.

Our business leaders and policymakers seem to ignore, completely, all of the credible research, data, and statistics that are readily available to everyone. Chapter 1 has outlined a complete rundown of the reasons we again find ourselves in survival mode much like the years following

"the Great Recession" instead of thriving like our large

business counterparts and Wall Street. It shows, through

this information, why the greatest country on earth is

destroying the American Dream one business and

community at a time, and, thus, the country as a whole.

Business SOS™ creates a sound argument for "thinking

big" and joining in a collaborative effort, focusing on our

small businesses. What Washington and Wall Street can't

or won't do for us we will have to do ourselves.

Since the start of 2020, more than two-thirds of US small

businesses have suffered tremendous losses with millions

of bankruptcies and scores of closures. I alone am not the

only one alarmed by these figures. With enormous

willpower, we simply cannot pull ourselves out of this

survival mode and back into growth. I have outlined how

this global pandemic and the speed of technology have

changed and overwhelmed small businesses across the country and how we need to harness this unique economic factor like our large business counterparts, collectively to help restore The American Dream and allow once more America to lead in our Capital markets. The implication of the research presented in this document is that by ignoring the true job creators and the soul of America, the middle class and small business, we will lose our power and stature in the world. The American brand as the "land of opportunity" will vanish.

Business SOS™ is a place—digital or otherwise—where struggling small businesses can go without recourse fear or shame to completely or partially redesign their business for the 21st Century. It is not an advice corner offering suggestions or consultation for a fee or a switch and bates but an open-source collaboration of resources through proprietary software for businesses in SOS.

It takes the disadvantages of facing less consumer demand, lack of capital, need to retool and enhance IT, modern effective marketing along with a variety of other critical components. It makes their acquisition and implementation obtainable—even while our economy continues to be in a downward trend with no growth.

Business SOS™ stops the merry-go-round and evaluates if these businesses can restructure to partake in the global market or perhaps retool to manufacture quality "American Made" goods and restore manufacturing jobs here, when appropriate. Instead of guessing we will solicit sponsors, experts, volunteers and staff who will coordinate these redesigns on a local, regional and national basis.

You will be able to interface with appropriate colleagues for partnerships to produce or sell in expanded markets. How we do this is through technology, but it also must be

287

done a crossed the board and to many businesses by awakening an economic nationalism and restoring true corporate governess and trust in our fellow colleagues. If we are to grow, we need to work together and trust each other once more. That is why when you sign a membership agreement it is not just riddled with indemnifications and protections on our behalf, but it is a two-sided real commitment to adhere to all of the rules of corporate governess and ethics. Values were offered symbolically on a handshake in decades past. This is a mandatory part of the membership, and this will be subject to the necessary ratings that review and digital data make so easy. You will know if his membership agreement and his score, reviews and history can trust the business offering service to you in advance. This will enable us to work faster in our quest to make these big changes rapidly, and before it is too late.

Small businesses need to be the "priority." We all admire Face book, Microsoft, Apple, and more. However, small businesses that can retool and grow against all the odds should be placed in value and in consumer and citizen consciousness.

There are many businesses out there that know they are already in SOS but facing it may be the biggest hurdle for so many of us. I know it was for me. Now there is a chance to do something about it.

What is the state of your company? Do you have the capital to hold on through this continued decrease and lack of confidence in consumer spending? What are your sales-to-debt ratio? How advanced is the hardware and software you are using? How are your sales? Sales and margins are the fuel to staying alive, and your very reason for being. Is your staff trained in the management and operation of all digital offerings?

How are your margins versus overhead and investment capital? How tech-savvy are you as the owner? How well trained is your staff?

How service-oriented is your accounting division? And how good are your product, service, and marketing? In today's world, it has to be 24/7 optimal service capability and production, which is the new normal. Can you keep up when the watchword is speed, speed, and speed?

These are some of the critical questions you need to ask to decide if you are in SOS and need an open-source of resources to help.

Can you maintain that "can do" attitude you had when you started, you're firm, or are you depressed and have the business blahs? Are you overwhelmed with all of the above? This is the nature of qualifying businesses for the services of Business SOS™.

Business SOS™ has just launched this progressive business model to do just that and will need time to grow organically. During this time, we are committed to helping one company at a time to redesign their business for the 21st Century. We offer an open-source of resources so that companies can advance their growth on their own.

Business SOS™ is one of many network resources available. We feel our point of difference is that we are not an advice corner but a way to actually implement the variety of changes a company would need to get out of SOS and back into a growth mode of operation. We expect others to develop, and we will create a website to house all of these resources. We are an inclusive business model, not an exclusive club. Everyone is invited to the party of reshaping America's small businesses.

There is only one word that describes many small businesses' understanding, adaptation, and knowledge surrounding the information technology revolution and that is "overwhelmed." I have presented a variety of comprehensive branding campaigns under my digital arm DJS 3SOP (three screens, zero paper) and found that most firms were aware of marketing online and through a variety of digital devices but very few had adequate knowledge of how to optimize these resources to meet their sales and marketing goals and objectives. They equated it to balls bouncing. They pick one up, and ten more are thrown their way. Which ones are right for them is anyone's guess from the analysis of most media plans for the average small business, the depth and results fall short. Seasoned CTOs with real knowledge are few and far between. I have tried to address what components are essential for establishing optimal digital marketing resources. The Business SOS™ website will categorize thousands of marketing firms and how to set up partnerships with them. We will establish guidelines to develop a first-class multimedia program and produce creative through this network of resources for various categories of industry and service sectors.

There is much to be reported that is bad, but there are also areas of opportunity that many small businesses have not been able to take advantage of due to the complexity of modern multimedia and the interface of the social networks. Never before in the history of small business is there a more cost-effective way to communicate and seek new customers from all over the world. Marketing is the most important tool to let people know you are out there, but it has radically changed since the year it began. We discuss in chapter 5 the relevance of three screens zero paper marketing. It explains all aspects of the Internet and mobile devices and the use of the Internet and social media on sales, growth, and branding. We intend to develop an online training center so that our network is up to date on all the new trends in media. Staying in front of your customer through these new media offerings is imperative. Mobile-first is imperative, but all three screens are important for small businesses to harness for inbound customer communication and sales.

Video is the fastest-growing tool to reach consumers in a compelling medium suited for dissemination a crossed all channels. Everyone is enticed to watch video on smartphones and tablets. The small business needs to have resources to produce their own video-on-demand and cost-effectively. Business SOS™ will provide the top resources in your area, or a crossed the globe that will help in the production and distribution of this new powerful marketing tool. No! Video is not just for large companies. It is now important to stream messages in this format if we are to keep up with viewer trends.

There are many reasons small businesses are in survival mode, many of which are not in the sphere of their corporate control. But one of the reasons the US finds itself in 1.2 percent growth is the lack of preparedness, education, and training for the quantum changes that have occurred recently to just about every business model that exists. There are profound changes in software and hardware, communication, finance, production, and more. Is your firm up to date on these changes and can you afford to retool? Are your marketing efforts capable of netting the consumer that will meet your growth goals? Is your physical plant capable of enhancing productivity? Just about every aspect of every business needs an overhaul in order to face the growth and competition challenges of 21st

Century business. How do we compare with operations in China, India, and Brazil? Our cultural thinking could be holding us back rather than economic circumstances. We need to borrow from the Olympic spirit of our American athletes and get back to competing and winning on the global stage.

Globalization assisted in removing barriers between nations through technology. However, it also resulted in competition for American jobs and manufacturing capability empowering countries like China, India, and Brazil. Globalization is moving very quickly and has changed the US competitive edge and flattened the playing field putting pressure on *all* businesses. Without formidable knowledge and pro-active, reliable methodologies, American small businesses are not taking advantage of the tremendous opportunities that globalization could afford them. It is obvious that American small businesses do not fully grasp this unique opportunity to lead in free trade.

This quantum change will require a whole new public

awaking and simplistic methodologies that will assist small

businesses in the repositioning of their businesses as not

just local or national, but "glocal." This, for some, maybe

the only way they can escape survival mode.

This *is* appropriate for our suburban and rural businesses

instead of geographic isolationism. We need to get in the

game of globalization before it is too late. We should be

providing leadership to the world in the global integration

of our industries and services. Business SOS™ will assist

all companies in their effort to understand how to transition

their firms for this kind of growth opportunity. This will

eliminate the time it will take to research and find the right

partnerships no matter what the need to expand your firm

globally. Whether it is production service or distribution,

our network intends to connect our businesses so that we

can achieve and take advantage of the tremendous opportunity to go global but avoid the pitfalls logistically and legally.

Business SOS™ is one of many network resources available. We feel our point of difference is that we are not an advice corner but a way to actually implement the variety of changes a company would need to get out of SOS and back into a growth mode of operation. We expect others to develop, and we will create a website to house all of these resources. We are an inclusive business model, not an exclusive club. Everyone is invited to the party of reshaping America's small businesses.

A love of country is the glue that binds us all together. We need to solve big, hard problems together and return to the ideals set forth by our forbearers that we are free individuals with a sense of community. If the top 1 percent is so adamant to keep their tax breaks let the remaining 99 percent do the hard work and sacrifice it will take to correct this horrible economic slide that has damaged the most advanced overachieving nation in the world. We need to redefine the brand that is truly American as "The land of opportunity for all and not just for a few." We must work together as a nation to advance progress.

By igniting a newfound inspiration of nationalism and service to our country, we will affect change one business and one community at a time. We will not let ourselves or our neighbors fail around us. We are a can-do nation. We get it done, but everyone needs to pull together, giving and doing whatever it takes. We will make it! We did it before, and we will do it again because this, in fact, is the greatest nation on earth. This is a result of love for our country and true nationalism. Washington is broken but not the spirit of everyday Americans.

Paying It Forward

We cannot solve our problems without a collective response. They are too big to be addressed alone. We are proposing that small businesses network together and reignite our nationalism and provide the catalyst to changing the forces that are impeding our progress. Business SOS™ can only provide the service of redesigning businesses by and through the help of other businesses. Their rewards for this help are knowing that they have done the right thing. We will be asking all of our businesses from sponsors, resources, networks and especially those that we assist in paying forward either through their product or service development or their own activism/volunteerism after they return to growth. We must change individual behavior as well as corporate largess to be based on collaboration and connectivity instead of secrecy, suspicion, and divisiveness. I believe all Americans understand the concept of freedom, capitalism, and its effect on corporate growth, progress, and prosperity. The sharing of prosperity by way of assisting our colleagues in learning, changing and growing nets tremendous fulfilment for us all as a nation. This fulfilment to help each other will result in the growth of our own GDP that should reward us all a crossed the board fairly.

Power and influence in the world will be maintained for future generations, and the possibility for a better life for all who participate in achieving these goals will be the results of this untold generosity. This is a large, ambitious task. But we, as a community, have faced much worse in our history and have worked together in our quest for resolution. We need the commitment and the will of all small businesses to help. Paying forward from our volunteers, sponsors, networked businesses, and organizations that jumped in to help each redesigned small business set the tone of 21st Century methodologies for growth.

Conclusion

We have outlined in this book the true state of small businesses today and what we believe will be the situation Post Pandemic. We have researched and exposed why this dysfunction continues and will continue and how we need to develop new methodologies to take many small businesses out of survival mode and back into growth. Identified are the key challenges for small businesses. First, managing the Corona Virus so that we take care of what matters most, our health and second, that we adjust to a completely digital and remote, automated world so that it enhances our businesses and avoids driving our small business to obsolescence.

How to Work Collaboratively so that We Capitalize on

this Unique Historical Moment Within the Constraints

of Our National Health Crisis and Financial Limitations

The substance of our network will measure us all. Business

SOS™ offers a vehicle to begin this process. It is driven to

redesign businesses within a framework that respects the

intellectual property of that business and the individual

owner. It will work to regain all of the business and

corporate governess that propelled our great nation in the

20th Century, such as honesty, integrity, fairness, good

work ethic, and quality of products and services. It will

place these high ideals in the new context of 21st Century

horizontal collaborative modalities and share with the

world what truly makes America the greatest nation in the

world. We need to stop being overwhelmed by these

quantum shifts in our marketplace and get back to meeting

these challenges with big ideas and methods that will keep

us competitive and in a position of leadership. We have an

incredible track record of building the world's most vibrant economy. We can, and we must succeed again at these endeavors. We offer our solution Business SOS™.

About Deborah Scarpa Founder and Author of

Business SOS™

Deborah Scarpa is an accomplished and experienced CEO and marketing expert across all platforms. As President of DJS3LLC, the company has accumulated a roster of national and international clients in a wide range of industries. Ms. Scarpa has a high-level, strategic business capability, along with marketing and management skills that have resulted in the proven success of DJS3 campaigns throughout the world. After the successful launch of her first book, *Business SOS™ Bring Back the American Dream*, published in the aftermath of the Great Recession of 2008, Deborah Scarpa expanded her communications offerings to include business consulting for R & D and development.

Ms. Scarpa's new digital arm has developed an innovative approach, and lead generating capabilities, in order for any business to determine their best multi-channel approach for today's marketing strategies with all forms of social media tailored toward glocal or global e-commerce. The current manuscript and the second edition of her book series called Business SOS™ Aftermath of a Pandemic was written in order to help bring back our lives and livelihood. It is a well-researched composition of current information critical to the survival of small businesses during and after the pandemic. It is a personal take on how to prepare for a post-pandemic America—focusing on greater adaptability of companies and a new, more durable domestic supply chain, along with how the rules we lived by no longer apply with a compelling glimpse into the new normal.

Business SOS™ is a place, digital or otherwise, that is a multi-channel, multi-platform methodology geared to help small businesses that are finding themselves incapable of adjusting to the quantum changes that are now occurring as a result of the worst public health crisis in modern history. She addresses the dire challenges for all businesses across the nation and the globe and supplys a human diary of a way forward. The mission of Business SOS™ is to help each small business that is in SOS and to offer the tools they need when they need them most.

Business SOS™ Books I and II can be found on Amazon, The Nook, Barnes and Noble, Library Thing, Goodreads, and all bookstore locations.

"Perhaps I did not receive a Harvard Business Degree, but starting several companies from nothing and turning them into multimillion, multinational corporations in the toughest economic times would qualify me for an honorary degree."

-- Deborah J Scarpa

[i] Harvard Business Review Collaboration. (2006, May). *Preparing for a Pandemic*. Harvard Business Review.
https://hbr.org/2006/05/preparing-for-a-pandemic
[ii] Harvard Business Review Collaboration. (2006, May). *Preparing for a Pandemic*. Harvard Business Review.
https://hbr.org/2006/05/preparing-for-a-pandemic
[iii] Schroeder, B. (2020, April 9). *Startup opportunities coming out of the pandemic—Some are opportunistic, others will be here for a long time.* Forbes.
https://www.forbes.com/sites/bernhardschroeder/2020/04/09/startup-opportunities-coming-out-of-the-pandemic-some-are-opportunistic-others-will-be-here-for-a-long-time/
[iv] Schroeder, B. (2020, April 9). *Startup opportunities coming out of the pandemic—Some are opportunistic, others will be here for a long time.* Forbes.
https://www.forbes.com/sites/bernhardschroeder/2020/04/09/startup-opportunities-coming-out-of-the-pandemic-some-are-opportunistic-others-will-be-here-for-a-long-time/
[v] Schroeder, B. (2020, April 9). *Startup opportunities coming out of the pandemic—Some are opportunistic, others will be here for a long time.* Forbes.
https://www.forbes.com/sites/bernhardschroeder/2020/04/09/startup-opportunities-coming-out-of-the-pandemic-some-are-opportunistic-others-will-be-here-for-a-long-time/
[vi] Jones, A. (2016). *Lesson Plan*. Course Hero.
https://www.coursehero.com/file/p11vk4j/Never-before-in-the-history-of-this-nation-have-so-many-human-and-property/
[vii] Hamer, G. (2020, April 13). *S.O.S. for small business*. Chamber Business News. https://chamberbusinessnews.com/2020/04/13/s-o-s-for-small-business/
[viii] Hamer, G. (2020, April 13). *S.O.S. for small business*. Chamber Business News. https://chamberbusinessnews.com/2020/04/13/s-o-s-for-small-business/
[ix] Hamer, G. (2020, April 13). *S.O.S. for small business*. Chamber Business News. https://chamberbusinessnews.com/2020/04/13/s-o-s-for-small-business/
[x] Hamer, G. (2020, April 13). *S.O.S. for small business*. Chamber Business News. https://chamberbusinessnews.com/2020/04/13/s-o-s-for-small-business/
[xi] Shen, J. (2020, April 4). *Cultivating adaptability is a pandemic coping skill*. Tech Crunch.

https://techcrunch.com/2020/04/04/cultivating-adaptability-is-a-pandemic-coping-skill/

[xii] Epstein, D. (2019). *Range: Why generalist triumph in a specialized world.* Macmillan.

[xiii] Shen, J. (2020, April 4). *Cultivating adaptability is a pandemic coping skill.* Tech Crunch. https://techcrunch.com/2020/04/04/cultivating-adaptability-is-a-pandemic-coping-skill/

[xiv] Maiiiikokookoollo. (2020). *Network 2008 notes.* Course Hero. https://www.coursehero.com/file/pcugnj8/With-software-so-many-potential-errors-can-be-made-that-simply-looking-at-past/

[xv] Liu, S., & Parilla, J. (2020, March 20). *What the Great Recession can tell us about the COVID-19 small business crisis.* Brookings. https://www.brookings.edu/blog/the-avenue/2020/03/25/what-the-great-recession-can-tell-us-about-the-covid-19-small-business-crisis/

[xvi] Liu, S., & Parilla, J. (2020, March 20). *What the Great Recession can tell us about the COVID-19 small business crisis.* Brookings. https://www.brookings.edu/blog/the-avenue/2020/03/25/what-the-great-recession-can-tell-us-about-the-covid-19-small-business-crisis/

[xvii] McKinsey & Company. (2020). *Coronavirus' business impact: Evolving perspective.* https://www.mckinsey.com/business-functions/risk/our-insights/covid-19-implications-for-business

[xviii] del Rio-Chanona, M., Mealy, P., Pichler, A., Lafond, F., & Farmer, J. D. (2020, May 16). *Predicting the supply and demand shocks of the COVID-19 pandemic: An industry and occupation perspective.* VOX EU CEPR. https://voxeu.org/article/industry-and-occupation-perspective-effects-covid-19

[xix] del Rio-Chanona, M., Mealy, P., Pichler, A., Lafond, F., & Farmer, J. D. (2020, May 16). *Predicting the supply and demand shocks of the COVID-19 pandemic: An industry and occupation perspective.* VOX EU CEPR. https://voxeu.org/article/industry-and-occupation-perspective-effects-covid-19

[xx] Zosche, C. (2020, July 30). *Spotify's listening audience increases after pandemic slump.* Adweek Network. https://www.adweek.com/blognetwork/spotifys-listening-audience-increases-after-pandemic-slump/78848

[xxi] Hsu, T. (2020, May 28). *The TV commercial, once advertising's main event, suffers in the pandemic.* The New York Times. https://www.nytimes.com/2020/05/28/business/media/coronavirus-advertising.html

[xxii] Ryan, R. (2020, May 27). *How the coronavirus is changing hiring and recruiting going forward.* Forbes.

https://www.forbes.com/sites/robinryan/2020/05/27/how-the-coronavirus-is-changing-hiring-and-recruiting-going-forward/#675294595ce4

xxiii Schmitt, B. (2007). *Big think strategy: How to leverage bold ideas and leave small thinking behind.* Harvard Business Review Press.

xxiv Willcocks, L., Venters, W., & Whitley, E. A. (2017). *Clear view of the cloud: The business impact of cloud computing.* London School of Economics.

xxv Tjemkes, B., & Pepign, V. (2012). *Strategic alliance management.* Routledge.

xxvi Willcocks, L., Venters, W., & Whitley, E. A. (2017). *Clear view of the cloud: The business impact of cloud computing.* London School of Economics.

xxvii Tjemkes, B., & Pepign, V. (2012). *Strategic alliance management.* Routledge.

xxviii Tjemkes, B., & Pepign, V. (2012). *Strategic alliance management.* Routledge.

xxix U.S. Department of Defense. (2020). *DoD Regulatory Program.* https://open.defense.gov/Regulatory-Program/Guidance-Documents/

xxx U.S. Department of Defense. (2020). *DoD Regulatory Program.* https://open.defense.gov/Regulatory-Program/Guidance-Documents/

xxxi Tice, C. (2012, January 4). *Six business trends to watch this year.* Entrepreneur. https://www.entrepreneur.com/article/222556.

xxxii Mull., A. (2020, May). *After the pandemic, the office dress code should never come back. The Atlantic.* https://www.theatlantic.com/magazine/archive/2020/05/kill-the-office-dress-code/609070/

xxxiii Mull., A. (2020, May). *After the pandemic, the office dress code should never come back. The Atlantic.* https://www.theatlantic.com/magazine/archive/2020/05/kill-the-office-dress-code/609070/

xxxiv Global Workplace Analytics. (2020). *Work-at-home after Covid-19—Our forecast.* https://globalworkplaceanalytics.com/work-at-home-after-covid-19-our-forecast

xxxv Global Workplace Analytics. (2020). *Work-at-home after Covid-19—Our forecast.* https://globalworkplaceanalytics.com/work-at-home-after-covid-19-our-forecast

xxxvi Global Workplace Analytics. (2020). *Work-at-home after Covid-19—Our forecast.* https://globalworkplaceanalytics.com/work-at-home-after-covid-19-our-forecast

xxxvii BBC. (2020, May 16). *How offices will change after coronavirus.* MyJoyOnline.com.

https://www.myjoyonline.com/lifestyle/relationships/how-offices-will-change-after-coronavirus/

xxxviii amBX Ltd. (2020, June 16). *What does the future office look like?* https://www.ambx.com/news/2020/6/15/future-office

xxxix Yon, M. K. (2020). *Understanding the business environment.* eLumine. https://elumine.wisdmlabs.com/courses/introduction-to-business/lessons/understanding-economic-systems-and-business/topic/understanding-the-business-environment/

xl OpenStax. (2018). *Understanding the business environment.* https://openstax.org/books/introduction-business/pages/1-2-understanding-the-business-environment

xli Gaskell, A. (2020, April 28). *Will we return to the office after COVID-19?* Forbes. https://www.forbes.com/sites/adigaskell/2020/04/28/will-we-return-to-the-office-after-covid-19/

xlii Volini, E., Schwartz, J., Denny, B., Mallon, D., Van Durme, Y., Hauptmann, M., Yan, R., & Poynton, S. (2020, May 16). *Returning to work in the future of work.* Deloitte Insights. https://www2.deloitte.com/us/en/insights/focus/human-capital-trends/2020/covid-19-and-the-future-of-work.html

xliii Volini, E., Schwartz, J., Denny, B., Mallon, D., Van Durme, Y., Hauptmann, M., Yan, R., & Poynton, S. (2020, May 16). *Returning to work in the future of work.* Deloitte Insights. https://www2.deloitte.com/us/en/insights/focus/human-capital-trends/2020/covid-19-and-the-future-of-work.html

xliv Sean. (2019, August 23). *Data-driven reasons why content marketing should be your next investment.* LYFE Marketing. https://www.lyfemarketing.com/blog/why-content-marketing/

xlv Patel, N. (2020). *What the coronavirus (COVID-19) means for marketers.* NeilPatel.com. https://neilpatel.com/blog/coronavirus/

xlvi Davis., S. & Toney, L. (2020, March 12). *How coronavirus (COVID-19) is impacting ecommerce.* ROI Revolution. https://www.roirevolution.com/blog/2020/08/coronavirus-and-ecommerce/

xlvii Howes, L. (2012, October 15). *7 tips for building a 'power network' on LinkedIn.* Entrepreneur. https://www.entrepreneur.com/article/224651

xlviii Whole Earth Provision. (2020). *Main Website.* https://www.wholeearthprovision.com/

xlix Kreik, S. (2019). *Summarize projected profits and key return metrics.* Course Hero. https://www.coursehero.com/file/p6lbeva/Summarize-projected-profits-

and-key-return-metrics-stabilized-yield-on-cost-IRR/

[l] Digital. (2019, February 18). *BigCommerce vs. Shopify – The Rivals.* https://digital.com/ecommerce-platforms/vs/bigcommerce-shopify/

[li] Pompa, M. (2020). *The results are in: The 22 best ecommerce website designs of 2020.* BigCommerce. https://www.bigcommerce.com/blog/best-ecommerce-website-design/

[lii] Wallace, T. (2020). *Need ecommerce business ideas? 27 experts give you their best online store opportunities for 2020.* BigCommerce. https://www.bigcommerce.com/blog/ecommerce-business-ideas/

[liii] Shahid, S. (2020, June 20). *50 top trending products to sell online at your ecommerce & dropshipping store in 2020.* CloudWays. https://www.cloudways.com/blog/trending-products-to-sell/

[liv] Deloe, J. (2018, November 27). *Top ecommerce niches of 2019.* eComDash. https://www.ecomdash.com/top-ecommerce-niches-2019/

[lv] Jacobs, R. (n.d.). *How to master product photography on a tight budget (we did it with less than $50).* BigCommerce. https://www.bigcommerce.com/blog/how-to-rock-product-photography-on-a-budget/

[lvi] Chambers, S. (n.d.) *How to write and promote a return policy customers love (includes example refund policies from real ecommerce businesses).* BigCommerce. https://www.bigcommerce.com/blog/create-a-returns-and-exchanges-policy-that-sells/

[lvii] Patch, L. (n.d.). *The complete guide to writing product copy that sells itself (+ 19 examples to get you started now).* BigCommerce. https://www.bigcommerce.com/blog/product-copywriting/

[lviii] Wallace, T. (2020). *Need ecommerce business ideas? 27 experts give you their best online store opportunities for 2020.* BigCommerce. https://www.bigcommerce.com/blog/ecommerce-business-ideas/

[lix] Pompa, M. (2020). *The results are in: The 22 best ecommerce website designs of 2020.* BigCommerce. https://www.bigcommerce.com/blog/best-ecommerce-website-design/

[lx] Estay, B. (n.d.) *The 11 most technically innovative ecommerce brands of 2020.* BigCommerce. https://www.bigcommerce.com/blog/innovative-ecommerce-brands/

[lxi] Estay, B. (n.d.). *Ecommerce store inspiration: Designs we love + sites with awesome functionality.* BigCommerce. https://www.bigcommerce.com/blog/best-ecommerce-stores/

[lxii] Estay, B. (n.d.). *Your guide to ecommerce themes: How to choose the right design for your online store.* BigCommerce. https://www.bigcommerce.com/blog/best-ecommerce-themes/

[lxiii] Jacobs, R. (n.d.). *How to master product photography on a tight*

budget (we did it with less than $50). BigCommerce. https://www.bigcommerce.com/blog/how-to-rock-product-photography-on-a-budget/

[lxiv] Patch, L. (n.d.). *The complete guide to writing product copy that sells itself (+ 19 examples to get you started now).* BigCommerce. https://www.bigcommerce.com/blog/product-copywriting/

[lxv] Wallace, T. (n.d.) *How to create ecommerce product videos that sell & convert (tips + examples).* BigCommerce. https://www.bigcommerce.com/blog/ecommerce-product-videos/

[lxvi] Wallace, T. (n.d.) *17 best ecommerce product video examples.* BigCommerce. https://www.bigcommerce.com/blog/product-video-marketing-examples/

[lxvii] Jones, C. (n.d.). *How to accept credit card payments online in 2020: What are your best options?* BigCommerce. https://www.bigcommerce.com/blog/how-to-accept-credit-card-payments-online/

[lxviii] Moore, K. (2020). *Payment gateways: Keeping your ecommerce transactions safe + customers happy.* BigCommerce. https://www.bigcommerce.com/blog/payment-gateways/

[lxix] Watson, C. (n.d.) *6 brands discuss how Amazon Pay increases their customer experience.* BigCommerce. https://www.bigcommerce.com/blog/amazon-pay-benefits/

[lxx] Wallace, T. (n.d.). *7 brands discuss the benefits of the new cashless economy and Apple Pay's growing ubiquity.* BigCommerce. nhttps://www.bigcommerce.com/blog/apple-pay-tips-mobile-payments/

[lxxi] Square Editorial Team. (n.d.). *6 surprising ways accepting mobile payments helps businesses.* Square. https://squareup.com/townsquare/6-surprising-ways-accepting-mobile-payments-helps-businesses

[lxxii] PNC. (2018, December 13). *8 things to know about payment security.* https://www.pnc.com/insights/small-business/running-your-business/8-things-to-know-about-payment-security.html

[lxxiii] Marsella, J. (n.d.). *Everything you need to know about achieving PCI compliance [checklist included].* BigCommerce. https://www.bigcommerce.com/blog/pci-compliance/

[lxxiv] Meyer, S. (n.d.). *What is ISO certification? ISO meaning and BigCommerce's ISO 27001 achievement.* BigCommerce. https://www.bigcommerce.com/blog/iso-certification/

[lxxv] Chambers, S. (n.d.) *How to write and promote a return policy customers love (includes example refund policies from real ecommerce businesses).* BigCommerce. https://www.bigcommerce.com/blog/create-a-returns-and-exchanges-policy-that-sells/

316

[lxxvi] Estay, B. (n.d.) *Next steps after the sale: Your guide to small business shipping.* BigCommerce. https://www.bigcommerce.com/blog/small-business-shipping-tips/

[lxxvii] Blanco, J. (n.d.). *Shipping rates 101: How to calculate shipping costs.* BigCommerce. https://www.bigcommerce.com/blog/calculate-shipping-costs/

[lxxviii] Dunn, J. (n.d.). *When and how to charge sales tax on shipping.* BigCommerce. https://www.bigcommerce.com/blog/shipping-sales-tax/

[lxxix] Lopienski, K. (n.d.). *Ecommerce fulfillment: The unappreciated yet vital strategy brands use to win loyal customers.* BigCommerce. https://www.bigcommerce.com/blog/ecommerce-fulfillment/

[lxxx] Overton, A. (n.d.). *Ecommerce shipping: Your step-by-step guide to shipping profitability.* BigCommerce. https://www.bigcommerce.com/blog/ecommerce-shipping/

[lxxxi] Lopienski, K. (n.d.). *How to maximize warehouse efficiency for your ecommerce merchandise.* BigCommerce. https://www.bigcommerce.com/blog/ecommerce-warehousing/

[lxxxii] Pekarek, L. (n.d.). *The truth about dropshipping: The good, the bad, and the ugly.* BigCommerce. https://www.bigcommerce.com/blog/dropshipping/

[lxxxiii] ShipBob. (2020). *Startup fulfillment services by ShipBob.* https://www.shipbob.com/startup-fulfillment-services/

[lxxxiv] Scarbrough, A. (n.d.). *30 proven ways to drive ecommerce traffic and conversions to your online store.* BigCommerce. https://www.bigcommerce.com/blog/how-to-drive-traffic-convert-customers/

[lxxxv] Wallace, T. (n.d.). *How to create ecommerce product videos that sell & convert (Tips + examples).* BigCommerce. https://www.bigcommerce.com/blog/ecommerce-product-videos/

[lxxxvi] Widmer, B. (n.d.). *Ecommerce SEO guide: How online stores can drive organic traffic in 2020.* BigCommerce. https://www.bigcommerce.com/blog/ecommerce-seo/

[lxxxvii] Mares, J. (2016, August 24). *How to use psychology & sales triggers to double your conversion rates.* Business 2 Community. https://www.business2community.com/ecommerce/use-psychology-sales-triggers-double-conversion-rate-01639207

[lxxxviii] Campbell, K. (2016, July 13). *Your primer to the psychology of marketing: The science of emotional buying and what marketers can do about it.* Business 2 Community. https://www.business2community.com/marketing/primer-psychology-marketing-science-emotional-buying-marketers-can-01594197

317

[lxxxix] Firuta, J. (n.d.). *Less sticking points, more sales: Actionable steps to remove friction from your buyer journey.* BigCommerce. https://www.bigcommerce.com/blog/remove-friction-buyer-journey/
[xc] Barbour, N. (n.d.). *3 Ways to Use Customer Data to Increase Conversions Right Now.* BigCommerce. https://www.bigcommerce.com/blog/customer-data-important-ecommerce/
[xci] Wallace, T. (n.d.). *31 ecommerce email marketing tips to 5x your conversion rates.* BigCommerce. https://www.bigcommerce.com/blog/ecommerce-email-marketing-strategy/
[xcii] Odziemek, K. (2017, November 30). *6 ideas for e-commerce land page. Tips, tricks and best practices.* Landingi. https://landingi.com/blog/6-ideas-e-commerce-landing-page-tips-tricks-good-practices
[xciii] Danesh, S. N., Nasab, S. A., & Ling, K. C. (2012). The study of customer satisfaction, customer trust and switching barriers on customer retention in Malaysia hypermarkets. *International Journal of Business and Management, 7*(7), 141-150.
[xciv] Sarcar, R. (n.d.). *How to set up an ecommerce loyalty program to improve retention, build community and drive 5x in sales.* BigCommerce. https://www.bigcommerce.com/blog/online-customer-loyalty-programs/
[xcv] Campbell, K. (2016, April 6). *3 phases of ecommerce personalization [part 1]: How to implement baseline site segmentation.* Business 2 Community. https://www.business2community.com/ecommerce/3-phases-ecommerce-personalization-part-1-implement-baseline-site-segmentation-01500285
[xcvi] Ferenzi, K. (2015, April 5). *Conversion rate optimization: Why this one metric determines your ecommerce success.* Business 2 Community. https://www.business2community.com/online-marketing/conversion-rate-optimization-one-metric-determines-ecommerce-success-01196868
[xcvii] Wallace, T. (2020). *The definitive guide to selling on Amazon [2020 edition].* BigCommerce. https://www.bigcommerce.com/blog/selling-on-amazon/
[xcviii] Wallace, T. (n.d.). *Using BigCommerce to sell on Amazon.* BigCommerce. https://www.bigcommerce.com/blog/selling-amazon-bigcommerce/
[xcix] Dennis. (2020, July 13). *Google shopping ads: The definitive guide (2020).* Store Growers. https://www.storegrowers.com/google-

shopping/

[c] Meert, B. (2017). *The complete guide to Facebook advertising.* AdvertiseMint.

[ci] Jeremy. (2020, July 27). *How to sell on Facebook.* Website Builder Expert. https://www.websitebuilderexpert.com/building-online-stores/how-to-set-up-a-facebook-store/

[cii] Spector, L. (2016, June 9). *How to grow an engaged, ready-to-buy community on Pinterest [checklist included].* Business 2 Community. https://www.business2community.com/pinterest/grow-engaged-ready-buy-community-pinterest-checklist-included-01562075

[ciii] Wallace, T. (n.d.). *BigCommerce customers can now sell on Pinterest across devices.* BigCommerce. https://www.bigcommerce.com/blog/pinterest-buyable-pins/

[civ] Wallace, T. (2020). *The complete guide to Twitter advertising for ecommerce businesses [2020 update].* BigCommerce. https://www.bigcommerce.com/blog/ecommerce-guide-to-twitter-advertising/

[cv] Barker, S. (n.d.). *How your business can make money selling on Instagram.* BigCommerce. https://www.bigcommerce.com/blog/how-to-make-money-on-instagram/

[cvi] Wallace, T. (n.d.). *Is Instagram shopping driving sales? The results are in: Brands report +1,416% traffic, +20% revenue.* BigCommerce. https://www.bigcommerce.com/blog/instagram-shopping/

[cvii] Estay, B. (n.d.). *Instagram influencer marketing: The organic superfood you need to fuel your ecommerce store.* BigCommerce. https://www.bigcommerce.com/blog/instagram-influencer-marketing/

[cviii] Sommer, C. (2012, February 22). *When you've got it - Flaunt it: A case study on Marie Forleo.* Forbes. https://www.forbes.com/sites/carisommer/2012/02/22/when-youve-got-it-flaunt-it-a-case-study-on-marie-forleo/

[cix] Gray, D. (2015, January 14). *Small business & the new FB algorithm.* LinkedIn. https://www.linkedin.com/pulse/small-business-new-fb-algorithm-deeann-gray

[cx] United States Courts. (2020). *About bankruptcy.* https://www.uscourts.gov/services-forms/bankruptcy

[cxi] United States Courts. (2020, January 28). *Bankruptcy filings increase slightly.* https://www.uscourts.gov/news/2020/01/28/bankruptcy-filings-increase-slightly

[cxii] American Bankruptcy Institute. *Newsroom.* https://www.abi.org/newsroom/bankruptcy-statistics

[cxiii] Epiq Systems, Inc. (2020). *Chapter 11 filings nationwide.*

319

https://abi-org-corp.s3.amazonaws.com/articles/aacer-jul-2020-commercial-bankruptcy-filings-all-chapters-ch-11-focus.xlsx

[cxiv] Mathur, A. (2007). *Forgive us our debts: New research finds that one of the best ways to encourage people to start businesses is to have lenient bankruptcy laws. Questia.* https://www.questia.com/magazine/1G1-158680920/forgive-us-our-debts-new-research-finds-that-one

[cxv] Mathur, A. (2007). *Forgive us our debts: New research finds that one of the best ways to encourage people to start businesses is to have lenient bankruptcy laws. Questia.* https://www.questia.com/magazine/1G1-158680920/forgive-us-our-debts-new-research-finds-that-one

[cxvi] Wikipedia. (2020, September 1). *Socialism.* http://en.wikipedia.org/wiki/Socialism

[cxvii] Wikipedia. (2020, August 10). *Endogeneity.* http://en.wikipedia.org/wiki/Endogeneity_(economics)

[cxviii] Wikipedia. (2020, August 29). *Corporatism.* http://en.wikipedia.org/wiki/Corporatism

[cxix] Wikipedia. (2020, September 1). *Entrepreneurship.* http://en.wikipedia.org/wiki/Entrepreneurship

[cxx] Mathur, A. (2007). *Forgive us our debts: New research finds that one of the best ways to encourage people to start businesses is to have lenient bankruptcy laws. Questia.* https://www.questia.com/magazine/1G1-158680920/forgive-us-our-debts-new-research-finds-that-one

[cxxi] Williams, V. (2016, July 29). *SNCC defends Black Lives Matter movement, which found a more receptive audience at the DNC.* The Washington Post. https://www.washingtonpost.com/news/post-politics/wp/2016/07/29/sncc-defends-black-lives-matter-movement-which-found-a-more-receptive-audience-at-the-democratic-convention/

[cxxii] GraduateWay. (2020). *Influence of immigration on the American culture and language.* https://graduateway.com/influence-of-immigration-on-the-american-culture-and-language/

[cxxiii] U.S. Department of the Treasury. (2020). *Main website.* https://home.treasury.gov/

[cxxiv] Purushothaman, D. (2013, December 13). *American ideals and values.* Living in Wellbeing. https://www.livinginwellbeing.org/american-ideals-and-values/

[cxxv] Lumen. (n.d.*) Reading: Small business and the U.S. economy.* https://courses.lumenlearning.com/ivytech-introbusiness/chapter/reading-small-business-and-the-u-s-economy/

[cxxvi] Bazerman, M. H., & Tenbrunsel, A. E. (2011 April). *Ethical*

breakdowns. Harvard Business Review. https://hbr.org/2011/04/ethical-breakdowns

[cxxvii] Koerner, B. I. (2011, February 28). *Made in America: Small businesses buck the offshoring trend.* Wired. https://www.wired.com/2011/02/ff-madeinamerica/

[cxxviii] Koerner, B. I. (2011, February 28). *Made in America: Small businesses buck the offshoring trend.* Wired. https://www.wired.com/2011/02/ff-madeinamerica/

[cxxix] Tolle, E. (1999). *The power of now.* Namaste Publishing.

www.ingramcontent.com/pod-product-compliance
Lightning Source LLC
Chambersburg PA
CBHW070525220526
45467CB00003B/852